Praise for
It Wasn't About Slavery

"A great read! Very informative, well written, and superbly researched. It brings out the truth behind the Civil War for those who can handle it. I recommend it highly."

> —**Phil Robertson**, author of *The Thief of America's Soul* and *Duck Dynasty* patriarch

"A number of good historians have lately published books challenging the American 'Myth of Righteousness'—the claim that the great War Between the States was all about freeing the slaves. It is juvenile to believe that so large and complicated a historical event as the U.S. government's massively destructive and revolutionary invasion and conquest of Americans of the South was, unlike every other war in history, entirely a matter of benevolence. Dr. Samuel Mitcham has nailed down this myth for all times for those who have the honesty to hear the evidence. If it was about one thing, the war was about *money*, the intent of the ruling elements of the North to keep their profitable control of Southern land and people. When the leaders of both sides made their plans and the soldiers of both sides went into battle, they were not thinking about the slaves."

> —**Clyde Wilson**, professor emeritus, University of South Carolina, author of a dozen books and 600 articles, editor of the twenty-eight volume *Papers of John C. Calhoun*, and founding dean of the Stephen Dill Lee Institute

"The minions of political correctness have been given a near death blow by Dr. Mitcham's latest book, *It Wasn't About Slavery*. Mitcham charges into the fray with a cartridge box full of truth and skillfully destroys the central element of the neo-Marxist assault upon the South. As Mitcham plainly demonstrates, regardless of which side of the Mason-Dixon Line America's heroes were born, the use of this 'politically correct' myth about slavery and the War Between the States is their starting point in attacking traditional American heroes. Mitcham's book, *It Wasn't About Slavery*, is more of a defense of traditional American heroes and values than a defense of the South."

> —**Walter Donald Kennedy**, author of *The South Was Right!*

"Dr. Samuel Mitcham's prowess as an author and a historian booms to the forefront in this book, *It Wasn't About Slavery*. In this age of politically correct history, which in reality is incorrect history, it is refreshing to find a noted historian who will not cower before the sycophants of false history. Dr. Mitcham's historical insight educates us, while his courage inspires us."

—Paul Grambling, Jr., commander-in-chief, Sons of Confederate Veterans

"In Dr. Samuel W. Mitcham Jr.'s *It Wasn't About Slavery*, the author presents a well-researched and thoroughly examined history of slavery in America that provides an unbiased and intelligent explanation of the real issues leading up to the Civil War—most importantly the long-accepted issue of slavery as the base cause of the War. Mitcham's research is eye-opening for the modern-day student of history who has too often been taught to believe that the evil of slavery only existed in the South, and that it was *solely* the North's attempt to abolish slavery that prompted the South to war. Mitcham picks apart this long-held belief and offers a clear, logical perspective on the *real* issues at the root of the Civil War and why the North branded slavery as the chief cause of Southern secession. Mitcham's compelling argument is a must read for those who long to know the *truth* about the institution of slavery in American history."

—Bridget Smith, author of *Where Elephants Fought*

"It has often been repeated that slavery was the cause of the War Between the States. Most who state this do so for political reasons. This aberrant notion has often been written about. Dr. Samuel W. Mitcham Jr.'s book *It Wasn't About Slavery* is a good historical documentation for the fact that some cannot face. The War, indeed, was not about slavery."

—Paul H. Yarbrough, author of *Mississippi Cotton* and *Thy Brother's Blood*

"Dr. Samuel Mitcham's new book has a title that's going to upset a lot of people—*It Wasn't About Slavery: Exposing the Great Lie of the Civil War*. To say this goes against the grain of popular culture is to make a gross understatement, but I would recommend you give the book a fair chance. You might not agree with everything he writes, but Dr. Mitcham makes his case that it was about money—or as I would say the same thing in another way, power. In an extensively sourced 179-page book, he lays out the entire history of the differences and frictions between the sections of the United States that together led to the most devastating war in its history. His book is a greatly needed corrective to current discourse and it is the 'rest of the story.'"

—Major General John Scales, author of *The Battles and Campaigns of Confederate General Nathan Bedford Forrest*

"Samuel Mitcham has dismantled the 'Myth of the Enlightened and Noble Federal Cause' and exposed the *real* origin of the 'War for Southern Self-Determination.' To gain a holistic view of the conflict, professional historians and history buffs alike must read this book!"

—**Kevin Adkins**, author and Civil War historian

"In his most recent book, *It Wasn't About Slavery*, Dr. Mitcham conveniently gathers into one place the relevant facts regarding the Civil War and slavery that took many of us years to find and digest on our own. If you want to understand *the war* and the current hysterical and increasingly violent response to Southern symbols, Southern monuments, and even Southern memory, here's your chance!"

—**Paul C. Graham**, author of *Confederaphobia: An American Epidemic* and *When the Yankees Come: Former South Carolina Slaves Remember Sherman's Invasion*

"Wow! Few authors today possess the intestinal fortitude to tackle highly controversial issues. Dr. Samuel W. Mitcham Jr. has done just that with his latest work, *It Wasn't About Slavery: Exposing the Great Lie of the Civil War*. Slavery did indeed play a role in the events leading up to the War Between the States. However, it turns out it was just one of many issues that led to the greatest conflict in the history of the United States. Dr. Mitcham, through extensive research, brings to light valid arguments that explain why the citizens of the southern states, nearly all of whom did not own slaves, were willing to risk everything and take up arms against the federal government.

Exploring constitutional issues such as nullification and the very act of secession, cultural differences, and the economies of both the North and the South, a valid argument is made that slavery was indeed a trigger, NOT the cause of the Civil War. In this age of revisionist history, this work stands alone as a must read for any true scholar committed to preserving the real history of the United States."

—**James Michael Pasley**, retired history professor and author of *Matt: Warriors and Wagon Trains*

"Samuel Mitcham has provided a great service to American history. The current attempt to reduce the causes of a complex war to slavery and only slavery is akin to middle school logic. No other historical event is given such a sophomoric treatment. Mitcham destroys this simplistic narrative and properly 'contextualizes' the most important event in our collective historical consciousness."

—**Brion McClanahan**, author of *Nine Presidents Who Screwed Up America: And Four Who Tried to Save Her*

"I was pleasantly surprised by this book on slavery and the Civil War. The book opens with quotes from Robert E. Lee and George Orwell on the topic of truth. The table of contents lists fifteen chapters followed by an extensive bibliography. In the introduction, the author summarizes his belief that the freedom of the slaves was not the cause of the war but the result of the war, and discusses how the root cause was money and the determination to not allow Southern self-determination. Of the numerous books I have read concerning the issue of slavery in America's Civil War, this is the most powerfully convincing and factual I've found. It is certainly a book that needs to be in every historian's library.

All the author's arguments are well illustrated with photographs and documented with quotes from primary sources, revealing his careful and extensive research. One favorite quote I found was by Jefferson Davis, president of the confederacy, who said, 'We are not fighting for slavery. We are fighting for Independence.' There are many other quotations the reader will find surprising. The author skillfully exposes the fallacies and distortions of truth behind those who rally behind the topic of slavery to attack the South. Mitcham also points out the racial prejudice that existed in the North. The historical anecdotes and epigraphs add much to illustrating Mitcham's arguments. The facts and quotations on secession are brilliantly presented.

For many years in my state history presentations at schools, libraries, and festivals, I have faced the stereotypical and historically ignorant beliefs that America's Civil War was started to end slavery in the South. Unfortunately, influenced by media and politicians, so many in my audiences do not want to know the real history and facts about slavery. This is a book I wish I had found years ago, and one which I intend to purchase in quantity and share with every university and secondary history teacher I can. If they will read and share Mitcham's finding and arguments with their students and peers, perhaps it will make a difference. This could be a life-changing book. I know it changed mine."

—Rickey Pittman, author of *Stonewall Jackson's Black Sunday School Class* and *Stories of the Confederate South*

"In the study of history, facts are sometimes very inconvenient things; they get in the way of pet theories. Professor Mitcham has presented those who insist that the War Between the States was caused solely by slavery with facts which can be ignored only at the price of intellectual dishonesty. The author demonstrates that more than one factor caused the conflict."

—Michael R. Bradley, professor emeritus, Motlow State, and author of *They Rode with Forrest* and *Nathan Bedford Forrest's Escort and Staff*

"When tyranny rules, truth becomes heresy. Sandy Mitcham's new book *It Wasn't About Slavery* will forever cast the author as villain and politically incorrect heretic because he dares to tell the truth—it wasn't about slavery."

—**James Ronald Kennedy,** author of *Punished with Poverty: The Suffering South* **and ten other books**

"This book is an intelligent, logical, and politically incorrect explanation of the causes of the War Between the States. The ex post facto explanations given by the winners to explain the war in strictly moral terms has relied on the historical ignorance of Americans—and it has worked. Having taught graduate history to military officers including those of other countries for years, the foreign officers understand this phenomena and many are brutal in their assessment of their fellow American students' inability to see truth. "The War Was Not About Slavery" is the unvarnished truth.

—**Lieutenant Colonel (ret) Edwin L. Kennedy Jr.,** **former assistant professor, U.S. Army Command and General Staff College, Fort Leavenworth, Kansas**

"In a provocative new book, noted Civil War historian Dr. Samuel W. Mitcham, Jr. answers the question rarely asked in American history classes: Was the Civil War fought to end slavery? His answer is no—it was the great lie of the Civil War.

No political party during the U.S. election of 1860 advocated freeing the slaves. In fact, at no time during his presidency did Abraham Lincoln free all the slaves; while during the war, he only freed slaves in southern secessionist states, which were not under Washington, D.C. control.

Instead of slavery, Mitcham writes that the Civil War was fought over money. Before the Civil War, the South financed most of the federal government, yet most of the federal subsidies and benefits went to the North. All the South wanted was limited government and lower tariffs—the ideals of Thomas Jefferson and other Founding Fathers.

Lincoln stumbled into the Civil War. He was unprepared for all the Southern states succeeding and had to find a way to bring them back to finance the federal government. Force was the only answer. So, the clever Illinois trial lawyer maneuvered the South into firing the first shot.

The result was an American tragedy and debacle. The South never recovered and, while finally freed, the lives of former slaves didn't improve. In fact, for many disease and death were the results of Union victory.

Compelling to read, Mitcham's book greatly expands our understanding of the Civil War."

—**Stephen Thompson,** historian and author

"This is a brilliantly written book showing the cultural and economic differences between the North and the South as the country was shaping and leading up to the War Between the States. Among these are the handling of laws and the shaping of the slave trade. Dr. Mitcham delves into the real causes of the war and the tactics of Mr. Lincoln. If you only read one book about the War Between the States this year, this should be the one."
—Christopher Rice, CEO, Confederate Broadcasting

It Wasn't About Slavery

It Wasn't About **Slavery**

Exposing the Great Lie of the Civil War

Samuel W. Mitcham Jr.

REGNERY
HISTORY

Regnery History™ is a trademark of Salem Communications Holding Corporation
Regnery® is a registered trademark of Salem Communications Holding Corporation

Cataloging-in-Publication data on file with the Library of Congress

ISBN 978-1-62157-876-5
ebook ISBN 978-1-62157-877-2

Published in the United States by
Regnery History
An imprint of Regnery Publishing
A Division of Salem Media Group
300 New Jersey Ave NW
Washington, DC 20001
www.RegneryHistory.com

Manufactured in the United States of America

10 9 8 7 6 5 4 3 2 1

Books are available in quantity for promotional or premium use. For information on discounts and terms, please visit our website: www.Regnery.com.

*Everyone should do all in his power to collect and dissemi-
nate the truth, in hope that it may find a place in history and
descend to posterity.*

—Robert E. Lee

*The further a society drifts from the truth, the more it will
hate those who speak it.*

—George Orwell

CONTENTS

INTRODUCTION

It is all very simple, the establishment historian writes: the Civil War was all about slavery. The selfless and morally superior Union soldier, brilliantly directed by a prophet and saint, Abraham Lincoln, invaded the evil and decadent South with no other purpose than to liberate the oppressed and downtrodden "Negro" from his cruel, sadistic masters. Filled with righteous indignation, these virtuous knights in military blue crushed the traitors and brought emancipation and heaven on earth to African Americans, all while bringing defeat and chastisement to the poor, ignorant Southerners, most of whom were slave owners or cruel overseers who wiped their noses on their shirt sleeves and chewed tobacco—even the women.

The victor, as Churchill said, writes the history, but these "historians" have abused the privilege. What passes for history today is cultural and intellectual nihilism, especially when it comes to the myth of the Enlightened and Noble Federal Cause. Their aim is not to seek the truth (which should be the ambition of every legitimate historian) but to serve an agenda. They are saying instead: "Forget the past unless it fits the narrative of which we approve because everything that occurred before us is irrelevant and inferior to our views and therefore should be forgotten, modified, 'corrected,' contextualized, or destroyed altogether."

Is it possible to be more narcissistic?

The French philosopher Bernard of Chartres remarked a long time ago that we stand on the shoulders of giants. Sir Isaac Newton made a similar pronouncement, but he added that the purpose was to see further—not to look down on the giants in scorn. I agree with Bernard and Sir Isaac and intend to teach history properly, standing on the shoulders of giants, seeing further, but not to erase or rewrite history into an "acceptable" form by looking down, in my case, on the American South. The primary purpose of this book is to help bring some balance to the debate about what happened in the pre-Civil War era.

First of all, I confess that I do not believe it was a "civil war." Most military schools outside the United States define a civil war as a struggle between two or more factions for control of the government. Establishment intellectuals have redefined the term in America in order to provide moral cover for what I call the the Lincoln regime. Yet if the standard international definition is accepted, one would have to conclude that the objective of Robert E. Lee, Stonewall Jackson, *et al.*, was to conquer and rule New York City, Chicago, Baltimore, Detroit and the rest of the North to label our 1861–1865 struggle a "civil war." This, of course, is absurd, though I dare say that all four cities, and many more, would have benefited immensely from a benign Confederate military dictatorship.

If we reject the term "civil war," what is a good name for the conflict? Some people prefer "The War of the Rebellion," favored by many Northerners in the nineteenth century. Others prefer "The War Between the States," while some refer to it as "The War for Southern Independence." Stonewall Jackson called it our "Second War for Independence." I prefer "The War for Southern Self-Determination," which it was, if we apply modern usage of self-determination. After all, if self-determination is good enough for Bosnia and Herzegovina, why isn't it good enough for Alabama and Mississippi? However, I will use the appelation "Civil War" in its place since it is widely understood and conforms to current usage, but it is nothing more than shorthand for "The War for Southern Self-Determination."

• • •

The War for Southern Self-Determination was not solely about slavery. Freeing the slaves was a *result* of the war, not the *casus belli*. In my view, slavery was part of a Cold War-like struggle between the North and South, whose economics, customs, religion, values, and ways of life were increasingly divergent. If culture is defined as the total way of life of a people, they had distinct cultures from the beginning. Only with the evolution of modern historical thought, heavily influenced by the ideas and tactics of Marx and Stalin, did the Civil War become "all about slavery." Marxist history validates the words of Confederate Major General Patrick Cleburne, who warned his men, "Surrender means that the history of this heroic struggle will be written by the enemy; that our youth will be trained by Northern school teachers their version of the war; will be impressed by all the influences of history and education to regard our gallant dead as traitors, and our maimed veterans as fit subjects for derision."

Legendary scholar Dr. Grady McWhiney agreed with General Cleburne over a century later. In 1980, he wrote, "What passes as standard American history is really Yankee history written by New Englanders or their puppets to glorify Yankee heroes and ideals."[1] My books are not puppets with New Englanders pulling the historical strings.

At this point, the reader might ask, if the Civil War wasn't about slavery, what was it about? The answer is simple: money. Most wars were and are about money or wealth transfer, including territorial acquisition, in one form or another. "What was slavery about?" Again, the answer is, money.

• • •

After the war, Admiral Raphael Semmes of the Confederate navy authored a book entitled *Memoirs of Service Afloat*. In it, he wrote that he did not anticipate Northerners would read his book because "men do not willingly read unpalatable truths... The people of America... like those best who fool them most, by pandering to their vices and flattering their foibles. The author, not being a flatterer, cannot expect to be much of a favorite...."[2]

The great captain was wrong in the case of his own classic, which has been in print since 1869. I hope this book enjoys a similar fate.

There are indeed indications of a return to balance and objectivity in the field of Civil War history. A new wave of scholars has arisen, and they are gradually restoring a degree of sanity to the mix. They include Clyde Wilson, Thomas DiLorenzo, Walter D. Kennedy, Donald Livingston, Karen Stokes, Kenneth M. Stampp, Jeffrey Hummel, Gene Kizer Jr., Biron McClanahan, James Ronald Kennedy, Frank B. Powell III, Paul Yarborough, John Emison, H. V. Traywick Jr., Leonard M. Scruggs, Paul C. Graham, John Taylor, John M. Taylor, James Rutledge Roesch, H. W. Crocker III, Walter Brian Cisco, Philip Leigh, Egon Richard Tausch, and the sages of the Abbeville Institute. The works of most of these fine authors are cited in this book and/or are listed in the bibliography. I hope that *It Wasn't About Slavery* will also find a place alongside the writings of these outstanding scholars.

I further hope *It Wasn't About Slavery* will be palatable to open-minded people on both sides of the old Mason-Dixon Line (although I am also aware it will make some people uncomfortable). I prefer to put my faith in the words of President Jefferson Davis, who said, "Truth, crushed to earth, is truth still, and like a seed will rise again."[3]

I should mention that there are some loose ends that I did not address in this book. Two of them are "Was secession treason?" and "Was Jefferson Davis a traitor?" Simply put, the answer to both questions is "No." Not one Confederate officer or official was tried for treason. Jefferson Davis, in fact, demanded a trial, but the victors refused to give him one. U.S. senator Charles Sumner (R-MA), one of the most hateful radical Republicans among many, deplored the fact that Davis was even captured because his presence in a Northern prison was a serious embarrassment to the government. They could not let him go because of Northern public opinion, but "to try him... would be the *ne plus ultra* of folly," Sumner wrote to Salmon Chase, the chief justice of the United States Supreme Court.[4] Chase agreed. He wrote to his former colleagues in Lincoln's cabinet in July 1866: "If you bring these [Confederate] leaders to trial, it will condemn the North, for by the Constitution secession is not rebellion."[5]

In the end, they had no choice but to release Confederate leaders. Even many moderate Northerners and some forgiving abolitionist leaders were demanding Davis' release. Finally, President Andrew Johnson (who personally despised Davis) yielded to the pressure and released Jefferson Davis on May 11, 1867. When the former Rebel commander in chief walked out of the courtroom in Richmond, a free man for the first time in two years, thousands of people (many of them black, it was reported) lined the streets and took off their hats in respectful silence.

●●●

Thanks, of course, are in order to everyone who helped with this project. Special thanks go to Walter D. Kennedy for his advice and for allowing me to use part of his library; to James R. Kennedy for his advice and reading an earlier version of this manuscript; to Dr. Clyde Wilson, General John Scales, and Colonel Ed Kennedy for reading an earlier version of this manuscript and making valuable suggestions for improvement; to Dr. Stephen Thompson for editing the final version and doing a great job; to Laura Swain for an excellent job at copy editing; to Elizabeth Kantor for assistance with photographs; to Donna Mitcham for editorial assistance, proofreading, and help in preparing this manuscript; and to Alex Novak, who came up with the idea for this book and honored me by selecting me to write it.

CHAPTER I

SLAVERY AND THE YANKEE FLESH PEDDLER

I believe that in the end truth will conquer.
—*John Wycliffe*

In his introduction to *To Live and Die in Dixie*, one of the best books ever written on Southern history and culture, R. Michael Givens noted that slavery was the glue that bound all anti-Southern arguments together. He also correctly pointed out that people are clueless as to the truth about slavery.[1] Though the Civil War was certainly not only about slavery, it was an issue. Now, it is an issue about which most people know next to nothing.

A poorly educated American believes slavery existed *just* in the Southern United States. However, it can be found in the first chapter of the Bible, in the Book of Genesis. The very word "slave" is ancient and comes from the word "Slav," the ethnic group that inhabits eastern Europe, including much of European Russia. And slavery continues to this day. According to the International Labor Office, a United Nations-affiliated organization, there were an estimated 40,300,000 slaves in the world in 2017.[2] This means that, in terms of raw numbers, there are *more slaves* in the world today than at any other time in history. There is, however, no great outcry about this fact, nor any large-scale movements to rid the world of it. After all, there is no money in that.

In ancient times, slavery was not based on race. It was based primarily on military conquest or bad luck. If you got in the way of the Roman army, for example, you would likely end up as a slave, or if you were the grandchild of someone who got in the way of the noble Roman, you would likely be born a slave. Slavery in its earliest days, therefore, was based on military conquest, though some people were enslaved because of financial debts.

Racial slavery began in the ninth century, when Arab Muslims began enslaving black Africans. The Arabs and Berbers, who were non-European Muslims, established the Trans-Sahara trade routes and took more than 10,000,000 Africans to North Africa and the Arabian peninsula.[3] They had to cross the Sahara Desert, and many died along the way. Some of these unfortunate Africans were captured as a result of aggressive military action. Others were sold into slavery by their fellow Africans. This era of the slave trade lasted until the nineteenth century.

The practice of slavery was accepted in many African societies even before the arrival of Muslims. It grew as many Africans converted to Islam and some of them went into the human trafficking business.

The second wave of race-based slavery began in the mid-1400s when Portugal established trading posts along the West African coast for the purpose of trading for slaves.[4] The slave trade was introduced into the New World by the Spanish in 1503. The British did not enter the business until 1562, but it was so lucrative that they soon wanted to dominate it. They were unsuccessful until 1713, when the Treaty of Asiento with Spain gave Great Britain the bigger share of the slave trade.

The American Yankee slave trade started on a modest scale in 1638. Boston began importing slaves for use in New England in a small way in 1644,[5] but not much else was possible. The slave trade was a Crown monopoly until 1749, when London opened it to all Englishmen. The New England elites saw the chance for enormous profits and were quick to seize the economic opportunity.

In *Captain Canot or Twenty Years of an African Slaver*, which was published in 1854, Theodore Canot provides us with some fascinating insight into the slavery business.

Canot was the son of a French officer and an Italian mother. He grew up in central Italy. His father died in the Battle of Waterloo, leaving his widow with six children to support. Canot, forced to drop out of school at age twelve, chose to go to sea. He apprenticed aboard the American ship *Galatea*, which sailed out of Boston, beginning in 1819. His first voyage was to Sumatra, Bengal, and Calcutta, among other places.

Young Canot lived a life of adventure. He apprenticed for five years, mostly doing business in the Indian spice trade. After escapades in Europe, he ended up in Paris, where he lost his money gambling. He took "French leave" from his hotel and secured employment with a British ship heading for Brazil. On the return voyage, he was shipwrecked. Then he boarded a Dutch vessel bound for Havana. After several more adventures, Canot boarded a clipper ship bound for Africa as an interpreter and supernumerary officer.

The clipper had a crew of twenty-one "scamps." Canot recalled, "… accustomed, as I had been, to wholesome American seamanship and discipline, I trembled not a little when I discovered the amazing ignorance of the master, and observed the utter worthlessness of the crew."[6]

After a forty-one-day voyage to Rio Pongo, Guinea, he and his captain faced an attempted mutiny; Canot and a loyal contingent put it down. During the struggle, Canot shot and killed one of the mutineers. The captain thought it best that Canot not return to Cuba, where he would face harsh Havana law. He stayed in Africa and went to work for a mulatto called "the Mongo" (a.k.a. Mr. Ormond), a local ruler and slave dealer. Many of the wealthy slave traders who dealt with the Mongo were Muslims, and Canot agreed to "follow the Prophet" for business reasons.[7]

While Canot was working for the Mongo, a Muslim slave trader named Ahmah-de-Bellah arrived with forty slaves. The Mongo accepted thirty-two of them and rejected eight. After some argument, Ahmah-de-Bellah consented to keep seven, which he likely slaughtered, but insisted that the Mongo accept the eighth because he (Ahmah) could neither kill him nor send him back.

Canot asked the chief what crime the slave had committed that he should be forced into permanent exile. Ahmah replied that this slave had killed his own son. There was no punishment in the Koran for a man who killed his son, so the judges of his country (Footha-Yallon) gave him a penalty they considered worse than death: he would be a slave to Christians for the rest of his life. On learning this, the Mongo accepted the killer as part of the bargain and resold him to Spanish slave dealers.

Before Ahmah-de-Bellah departed, he told the Mongo that his father, Ali-mami, intended to launch a "great war" the following year on a variety of smaller, non-Muslim tribes. He would expand his animal herds and have many more slaves to sell Ormond. Canot learned that Sharia law prohibited Ali-mami from making slaves of Muslims but had no restrictions for non-believers. He also learned that African chieftains in the interior were fond of working their slaves until their bodies were about to fail; then they would try to sell the worthless slaves to white men who had established trading outposts on the African coast.[8]

Theodore Canot finally became captain of his own slave ship, the schooner *La Fortuna*, in March 1827. It included a cargo of 200,000 low-quality cigars, 500 ounces of Mexican gold, and 220 slaves. Three months later, in northern Cuba, he sold the slaves for $77,469 and the vessel for $3,950. After expenses, his net profit was $41,438.[9] According to the U.S. Bureau of Labor Statistics consumer price index, $41,438 in 1827 is worth over $915,000 today, after inflation is factored in.[10]

These figures make it easy to see why New England businessmen embraced the slave trade so readily. In 1836, English Captain Isaacs visited the slave trading port of Lamu on the island of Zanzibar. It was overrun with Northern flesh peddlers. "There were so many Yankee slavers and traders active in Zanzibar that the local population thought that Great Britain was a subdivision of Massachusetts," Isaacs recalled.[11]

All U.S. slave ships were built in the North; none were constructed in the South. Their crews were mostly Northern men, and Northerners prospered by the trade. New England also prospered indirectly because their capitalists bought Southern goods that were mostly produced by slaves. The Yankees then sold them overseas, usually at a handsome profit. The centers of the slave fleets were not New Orleans, Charleston, or Savannah. They docked at Boston, Massachusetts, and Providence, Rhode Island, later joined by New York City, which was also the financial center of the slave business. New York bankers loaned money to slave buyers and Southern plantation owners to expand their cotton acreage. They often accepted slaves as collateral.

New England quickly developed a "Triangle Trade." Yankee sailors loaded their slave ships in a New England port with fish and rum. They then sailed to Africa, where they exchanged the rum for slaves. The usual rate was about 200 gallons per slave. Next, they sailed to the West Indies, where they traded the slaves for gold and molasses. After this, they returned to New England, where they sold the molasses to distillers so that they could make more rum. Sometimes they stopped at a Southern port and delivered blacks to auctioneers. This was only a minor part of their business. Only six percent of the slaves exported from Africa to the New World were destined for the thirteen American colonies. The bulk of them went to the Caribbean, West Indies, Brazil, or the sugar plantations of South America or the islands such as Trinidad and Tobago.

When the British Parliament tried to collect a tax on molasses, the Massachusetts merchants were upset. They protested that the tax would ruin the slave trade and cause more than 700 ships to be docked for lack of work. It would result in high unemployment in the rum business. There were sixty-three distilleries in Massachusetts producing 12,500 hogsheads of rum. (A hogshead is a barrel holding 63 to 140 gallons.) There were another thirty-five distilleries in Rhode Island.[12]

By 1703, slavery was a respected institution in the North. More than 42% of New York City households owned slaves. This was the second highest total of any city in the thirteen colonies, surpassed only by

Charleston, South Carolina.[13] They were primarily employed as domestic servants and laborers. Other slaves toiled as agricultural laborers in the fields of Long Island, the Hudson Valley, and the Mohawk Valley. In 1711, the first slave market started on Wall Street, near the East River, and ran for fifty-one years.

The Northern flesh peddlers obtained their black chattels primarily from other Africans. Historians Linda Heywood and John Thornton of Boston University estimated that 90% of the slaves shipped to the New World were first enslaved by Africans and only later sold to Europeans and Americans. Professor Henry Louis Gates Jr., of Harvard University writes: "The sad truth is that without complex business partnerships between African elites and European traders and commercial agents, the slave trade to the New World would have been impossible, at least on the scale it occurred."[14] Gates points out that the present-day advocates of reparations ignore this "untidy problem" and want people to believe the romanticized version—that all the ancestors of present-day African Americans were kidnapped by evil whites, as portrayed in the abduction of Kunta Kinte in *Roots*. "The truth, however, is much more complex," Gates writes, saying, "slavery was a business, highly organized and lucrative for European buyers and African sellers alike."[15] The Fon (ruler) of Dahomey (now Benin), the Akan of the Kingdom of Asante (now Ghana), the Mbundu of Ndongo (now Angola), the King of Bonny (present day Nigeria), and the Mbundu of the Kongo (Congo) were just a few of the larger African slave dealers. King Gelele of Dahomey told Britain's Sir Richard Francis Burton that God ordained the slave trade. "If I cannot sell my captives taken in war, I must kill them," he told the horrified diplomat and naval captain, "and surely the English would not like that." Chief Gezo of the same kingdom later told Sir Richard: "The slave trade is the ruling principle of my people. It is the source of their wealth... the mother lulls the child to sleep with notes of triumph over an enemy reduced to slavery."[16] Frederick Douglass used this fact as an argument against repatriations, stating that the "savage chiefs of the western coasts of

Africa" were no more inclined to accept abolitionist moral ideas than the American slave traders.[17]

Slavery grew throughout the United States in the eighteenth century. In Connecticut, for example, one-half of all ministers, lawyers, and public officials owned slaves, and one-third of all doctors had them as well. Nearly all the principal families of Norwich, Hartford, and New Haven possessed, it was said, one or two slaves. Being a free black person in that colony was no picnic, either. By 1690, no blacks or Indians could be out on the streets after nine o'clock at night, and they could not go beyond their town limits without a pass. In 1708, there were frequent fights between whites and blacks. The colony passed a law whereby any black person who disturbed the peace or even tried striking a white person for whatever cause would receive thirty lashes. Twenty-two years later, even speaking against a white person could draw forty lashes for any black, Indian, or mulatto.[18]

In 1717, the Connecticut Colonial Assembly passed a law forbidding free black or mulattos from living in any town without that town's permission. Nor, the law said, could they own land or a business without the town's approval. This provision was retroactive.[19]

By the end of the American Revolution, slavery was found throughout New England. The descendants of the Puritans had no qualms about enslaving people whom their religious leaders described as savages. In 1783, one out of every four families in Connecticut owned slaves, and one out of every fourteen people in Rhode Island was a slave.[20] Some of the most prominent men in the North were involved in the slave trade, including John Hancock (first signer of the Declaration of Independence, governor of the Commonwealth of Massachusetts, and a significant slave trader) and Josiah Franklin (Benjamin's stepbrother and a prominent Boston slave dealer). Prominent Northern supporters of slavery and/or slave owners included Cotton Mather (the prominent Puritan minister); Judge John Saffin (a New England poet who, ironically, argued against slavery); General Jacob Herkimer (a Revolutionary War hero from New York); Frederick Muhlenberg of Pennsylvania (the first speaker of the U.S. House of

Representatives); Samuel Huntington of Connecticut (a signer of the Declaration of Independence, president of the Continental Congress [1779-81], and later governor of Connecticut); Stephen Hopkins (signer of the Declaration, governor of Rhode Island, and chief justice of the state supreme court); Sam Adams (Founding Father and cousin of President John Adams); U.S. Senator and Revolutionary War general Peter Muhlenberg of Pennsylvania; and even Benjamin Franklin (Franklin later had a change of heart and founded one of the first anti-slavery societies on the North American continent, but he held slaves as late as 1781).[21] His great-great-grandson, Captain Temple Franklin Cooper, served in the Confederate Army and died in a Union prison camp.[22] Most of the people listed above based their arguments in favor of slavery on the Bible.[23]

During the slave trader era, Northern and European flesh peddlers transported 24 to 25 million black people from Africa to the New World. Between 4 and 5 million of them died *en route* (the so-called "Middle Passage"), primarily because of the brutality of the slavers.[24] But history was making one of its periodic turns. The Age of Enlightenment dawned, and with it arrived the idea that slavery was wrong—or at least the idea garnered widespread global acceptance for the first time. Led by the British clergy, and famously by layman evangelist and member of Parliament William Wilberforce, much of the world renounced human bondage and embraced the idea of compensated emancipation. Even so, the North remained linked to slavery. Much of the capital that propelled the Industrial Revolution came from the slave trade. The North continued to profit from and, in one form or another, promote slavery until 1861. It also reaped massive financial benefits from federal tariffs on imports. (A tariff is a tax or duty placed on imports and/or exports.) Slavery and the commodities it produced for export, in fact, funded most of the federal government as late as 1860.

●●●

Today, white Southerners are sneered at and ignorantly blamed for inventing slavery. There were in fact five main groups involved in the second great era of racial servitude (i.e., the era of the European and American slave trader): 1) Africans; 2) Arab-Muslim slave traders; 3) Northern flesh peddlers and other Yankees; 4) Latin American plantation owners; and 5) Southerners. In modern times, far too many people "give a pass" to everyone except the Southerner—often without realizing it. This trend is a grievous injustice. The morally superior, sanctimonious attitude some people adopt when lecturing others concerning the sins of their ancestors isn't factual. When it comes to America's "peculiar institution," there is plenty of guilt—if that is the objective—to spread around.

CHAPTER II

HYPOCRISY

Truth is deathless.
—*Admiral Raphael Semmes, C.S.A.*

By 1750, there were three times as many slaves in Connecticut as there were in Georgia. Massachusetts had four times as many as the Peach State.[1]

Northerners never particularly liked black people prior to the Civil War. New York City was one of the centers of the Northern wing of the "peculiar institution," and the colonial Big Apple had its problems with it too. In 1741, several fires broke out in the city, including one in the lieutenant governor's house. Further investigation into the fires uncovered the "Conspiracy of 1741," also known as the Negro Plot of 1741 or the Slave Insurrection of 1741. Those believed guilty were quickly arrested. More than two hundred people, including twenty poor whites, were jailed while more than a hundred were hanged, exiled, or burned at the stake. The two black leaders were gibbetted (i.e., hung in chains in a public display and left to die of exposure, thirst, and starvation). At least thirty-eight slaves faced execution along with several whites. Fourteen blacks were burned at the stake.[2]

As soon as the labor supply in the North became enough to reduce the cost of white labor (which it did through immigration and high birth rates), the Yankees began to cut down on their number of slaves. By 1776, Georgia had more slaves than New York, which still had more than 10,000. Georgia had around 15,000 chattels.[3] Most of them were employed as domestic servants or in rice production.

The Pennsylvania legislature enacted a gradual emancipation act in 1780.[4] Five years later, the New York Manumission[5] Society was established. The state passed a progressive abolition law in 1799, with the goal of ending slavery by 1827. Rhode Island also passed a manumission law, but it was very carefully written to protect the slave trade, which enriched the state.[6] All of the Northern states had enacted anti-slavery legislation by 1830. The Northern manumission and emancipation laws were designed so that the slaves' masters did not lose money. The laws always had a liberation date. If a slave was born before that date, he would be a slave the rest of his life unless he successfully escaped or was freed by his "Massa." If a slave was born after that date, he would be freed on his twenty-first birthday—at least in state law. "Massa," however, could always sell his slaves south before the liberation date. If the law said that a slave would be liberated on his twenty-first birthday, for example, the black person could be pretty confident that he would celebrate that birthday in a tobacco field in Virginia or a rice paddy in South Carolina. There was no moral outrage against slavery in the North. Much of the impetus behind manumission was a desire to protect white labor from cheap black competition.

Even after the blacks were freed, they were unwelcome in the North. This fact is reflected in the declining population of Northern blacks in relation to whites. The censuses from 1790 to 1830 show a decline in the free black population of New York from 2.13 percent to 0.57 percent. One reason was kidnapping. Many faced the prospect of being kidnapped and sold into slavery. There were. for example, thirty-three reported kidnappings of black people in New York City alone in a single year.[7]

The most famous kidnapping victim of the antebellum period was Solomon Northup of Sarasota Springs, New York. Northup was not only a very intelligent man with a wife and family, he was also a skilled violinist. When he was thirty years of age, two men from New York state induced him to come with them to Washington, D.C., to play his violin for a circus. Once in the capital, they fed him a drug that knocked him out. He woke up a slave and was soon on his way to Louisiana.

Northup tells both the good and bad of slavery. He describes how one woman suffered when both of her children were taken from her. She had already lost her son when he had been purchased earlier. The man who bought her did not want her daughter. She cried, pleaded, and begged, and touched the heart of the slave-buyer. He offered to buy the little girl whom he did not need (in what Northup called an act of humanity), but the slave trader had become so annoyed with her that he refused to sell the child at any price. The mother thus lost both her children and eventually died of a broken heart.

Northup was initially fortunate in his masters: " ... there never was a more kind, noble, candid, Christian man than William Ford," he wrote. "... A model master, walking uprightly, according to the light of his understanding, and fortunate was the slave who came to his possession. Were all men such as he, Slavery would be deprived of more than half its bitterness."[8] Unfortunately, Ford signed a note for his brother, who defaulted. Ford came under a large judgment and had to sell his servants, including Northup, to a cruel and unjust master named Tibeats. One day, when Tibeats tried to beat Northup with a whip, the slave took the lash from the master and struck him with it several times. This act almost cost the slave his life. Tibeats left and returned with two other men intent on killing the African American. The noose was already around Northup's neck when Mr. Caplin, Ford's overseer, approached the lynch party with a brace of pistols. Mr. Ford kept a $400 mortgage on Platt (Northup's slave name), Caplin declared, and he would shoot the man who tried to hang him. (This was a pretext. Northup never thought his salvation was about money.) This ended the attempted lynching.

On another occasion, Tibeats attacked Northup with a hatchet. The slave took it from him and gave him another severe beating. This time, neither Ford nor Caplin were around, so Northup fled into the Great

Pacoudrie Swamp pursued by bloodhounds. He was fortunate that he had become a good swimmer in New York. (Louisiana slaves were never taught how to swim. If you were a slave in south Louisiana and could not swim, there was no way you were going to escape.) He was doubly fortunate water moccasins did not bite him. They were everywhere in the swamp, as were alligators. He eventually made his way back to Mr. Ford's and safety.

Mr. Ford told Tibeats to sell Northup, which he did. (In the South, in those days, people with enough standing in the community could issue orders to white trash and have them obeyed, whether they had any legal right to give those orders or not.) Northup's new master wasn't bad when he was sober—which wasn't all that often. When he was drunk, he was a sadist. He liked to chase his slaves and beat them with a whip, laughing uproariously as they screamed. But at least it wasn't a hatchet.

Northup was a slave for twelve years, mostly on sugar and cotton plantations. Eventually, he overheard Samuel Bass, a prominent white citizen of Marksville, Louisiana, fiercely denouncing slavery as a moral wrong. Northup secretly told Bass that he was a free black kidnap victim. Bass wrote letters to New York, which eventually led to his release.

When he returned to New York, Northup sued the men who kidnapped him and the Washington, D.C., slave dealer. They filed legal delays in the Northern state and were never punished. "It is but justice to say, that the authorities at Marksville, cheerfully rendered all the assistance in their power," "Platt" wrote later. When he returned, Northup penned a wonderful book, *Twelve Years a Slave*, telling the truth about slavery. It was called "Uncle Tom's Cabin Number Two." It is vastly superior to *Uncle Tom's Cabin*. If you go to the library, you will find it in the non-fiction section. Unlike *Uncle Tom's Cabin*, it really happened. Sadly, Solomon Northup died in poverty, unable to profit from his experience.[9]

● ● ●

During the antebellum period, none of the Northern states allowed black people to vote, but some states were more restrictive than others.

New Jersey, for example, passed a law forbidding the importation of African Americans (free or slave) into the state in order "that white labor may be protected."[10] Massachusetts allowed blacks into the state, but by law, any black who remained longer than two months was to be punished by public flogging.[11]

From the end of the Revolutionary War until the 1830s, excepting a small minority, there was no moral outrage against slavery in the North. Only later did Northern leaders decide slavery was a terrible sin.[12]

Slavery was more economically entrenched in the South after the War for American Independence, but the revolution's ideological fervor against any form of human bondage made significant inroads even there.[13] Then, in 1793, Eli Whitney invented his cotton gin.[14] Now, instead of painstakingly cleaning a pound of cotton per day by hand, a single slave could gin fifty pounds of cotton per day without tearing the fiber. The potent combination of cotton, an efficient gin, the development of the Petit Gulf strain of cotton,[15] and slavery led to an explosion in the production of "White Gold." Southern cotton production increased from 5 million pounds a year in 1793 to 500 million in 1835, and it made quite a few Southern plantation owners rich. Naturally, the demand for field hands soared.

The South was now going against the flow of history. After centuries, much of the rest of the world had decided there was something morally wrong about human bondage. The British abolished the slave trade in 1807, and Wilberforce and his many allies began to campaign for a complete emancipation and the end of slavery itself throughout the globe. Even in the labor-intensive sugar plantation countries of Brazil and Cuba, the number of free blacks was approaching the number of slaves. In Mexico, for example, manumission had practically ended slavery long before it was formally abolished in 1829.[16] The United States outlawed the slave trade in 1808. Southern senators and congressmen supported this measure.

Even though the slave trade was now illegal, the Northern flesh peddlers continued to sail and rack up the profits with tacit support from the United States government. Great Britain and France wanted to stop the illicit trade, so they asked for permission that their agents board and search American vessels for human cargo. President John Quincy Adams of Massachusetts denied this request. The European powers did not want to board American vessels without permission, (i.e., they did not want to risk a war), so the U.S. flag proved to be ample protection for slave traders. They continued to operate until 1885 (twenty years after General Lee surrendered) when Brazil became the last nation to end the importation of slaves.[17] The attitude of the flesh peddler was perhaps best expressed by the other John Brown, a rich slave peddler for whom Brown University in Rhode Island is named (not to be confused with the terrorist hanged in 1859). When he was criticized for traveling to Africa to bring back slaves, he replied that "there was no more crime in bringing off a cargo of slaves than in bringing off a cargo of jackasses."[18]

Nor did the official closing of the slave trade slake the Northern greed for profit or the planters' lust for cheap labor. In 1859, less than two years before the events at Fort Sumter, U.S. naval warships captured eleven slavers.[19] Writing for the Abbeville Institute, esteemed historian H. V. Traywick Jr., outlines the testimony of the last known individual illegally smuggled into the United States before the Civil War. His name was Cudjo "Kossola" Lewis, and his story can be found in *Dust Tracks on a Road* by noted African-American anthropologist Zora Neale Hurston.[20]

As Traywick describes, Kossola was a member of the Takkoi nation in West Africa, and their compound was attacked one morning by the Amazon women warriors of Dahomey. They beheaded the old and sick and carried their heads off as trophies. The rest were marched in a slave column to barracoons (slave barracks) on the beach at Dmydah. The Dahomians stopped on the second day to smoke the heads of their decapitated victims because they began to stink.[21]

Jailed in barracoons, survivors of the ordeal awaited arrival of a slave ship. Tribes were separated from each other—Dahomians were afraid they would fight one another despite enslavement together. The ship was the *Clotilda*, sailing out of Maine. The slave trader chose the people he wished to buy and set sail for the United States. Because it was now illegal, the slave ships were built for speed. A British man-of-war chased it, but the slaver outran it. The *Clotilda* reached Mobile and sailed upriver, where it unloaded its cargo of some one hundred human beings. The owner then scuttled the ship.[22]

Kossola was luckier than most. Because of the war, his career as a slave was short. He and his people created the settlement of Plateau, Alabama, and some of their descendants live there to this day.

In *The Suppression of the African Slave Trade to the United States*, famed African American historian and Harvard professor W. E. B. Du Bois quoted the New York *Journal of Commerce*, which stated that New York was the largest African slave-trading port in the world in January 1862, followed by Portland, Maine, and Boston, Massachusetts. The eighty-five slave ships sailing out of New York transported 30 to 60 thousand slaves from Africa annually.[23]

Zora Neale Hurston, a prominent African American writer and anthropologist, said that it "stuck in my craw" that her own black people had sold her ancestors into slavery. She had been raised on stories that white people had gone to Africa and lured the Africans onto the slave ships by waving a red handkerchief. When they boarded the ship to investigate, it sailed away with them. But, no, she declared, her own people had "butchered and killed, exterminated whole nations and torn families apart, for a profit." She was sadly impressed with the "universal nature of greed and glory."[24]

CHAPTER III

SECESSION: THE CONSTITUTIONAL ISSUE

The principle, on which the war was waged by the North, was simply this: That men may rightfully be compelled to submit to, and support, a government that they do not want; and that resistance, on their part, makes them traitors and criminals.[1]

—Lysander Spooner, abolitionist leader

The noted historian Shelby Foote was right: those who say that the war was all about slavery are just as wrong as those who declare that the war had nothing to do with slavery.[2] The fake historians and purveyors of the myth of the Noble and Enlightened Cause to end slavery willfully ignore other causes, including huge constitutional issues, such as secession, nullification, and judicial overreach, which led Thomas Jefferson to refer to the judiciary as "a despotic branch."[3] They also ignore a central question that was settled by violence in 1865 but that often dominated the public debate from 1776 to 1861: what kind of government would we have? There are also a number of other questions and concerns that had to be addressed then and have to be addressed now.

The issue of secession can be dealt with very simply. The United States was the product of secession. The Declaration of Independence was the most beautiful Ordinance of Secession ever written.

Even before it won the Revolutionary War, the U.S.A. was governed by the Articles of Confederation (1781–1789). The statesmen who authored it believed the thirteen individual states were and should remain sovereign. They wanted a highly restricted federal government, and in that lay the problem: they limited it so much that it was ineffective. It did not even allow for a chief executive office (i.e., a president). When the American ambassador to Paris proposed a treaty, the French foreign minister asked how many treaties would there be: one or thirteen? Another flaw lay in the Confederation's preamble, which declared that the Articles created a "perpetual" union.

Because the Confederation was so ineffective, every state left or seceded from it by 1790, regardless of what the preamble said. They held a Constitutional Convention, beginning in Philadelphia in 1787. After considerable wrangling, the Constitution of the United States went into effect on March 4, 1789. The concept of a perpetual union was conspicuous in its absence.

Every state (colony) recognized the right of secession in 1776 and again in 1789. The Constitution dealt with this right indirectly in Amendment Ten of the Bill of Rights, which states: "The powers not delegated to the United States by the Constitution, not prohibited by the States, are reserved to the States respectively, or to the people." It was ratified by the states between 1789 and 1791 and added to the Constitution on December 15, 1791.

New York, Rhode Island, and Virginia did not wait for the addition of the Tenth Amendment to the Constitution to ensure they could leave the Union if they wished. They explicitly reserved the right to secede when their legislatures ratified the Constitution on July 26, 1788; May 29, 1790; and June 25, 1788, respectively.

Lawyers and politicians, of course, are experts at twisting any clearly written sentence to mean whatever they want it to mean, and they later did so with the Constitution in general and the Tenth Amendment vis-à-vis secession in particular. Entire books have been, and will be, written on this topic, but the absence of any mention of secession in the Constitution and the intent of the Tenth Amendment remain quite clear. There is no need to waste any of our time on some prattling lawyer's intellectual break dancing!

The Founding Fathers, led by Thomas Jefferson and James Madison, established a government based on a system of checks and balances. Foremost, they wanted to check and balance the power of the central government. Not everybody agreed. Alexander Hamilton led a group (later a political party) called the Federalists, which advocated a strong central government ruling over an essentially commercial state, a national bank controlling the currency, a president with almost royal powers, a Senate elected for life, and a system of protective and revenue tariffs. Jefferson and his followers, on the other hand, preferred an agrarian-based limited government. The argument between Hamiltonians (large, strong, central government) and Jeffersonians ("governs best which governs least") continues—albeit in altered form—to the present day.

● ● ●

"The Union," Dr. Donald W. Livingston wrote, "had never been happy."[4] As early as 1794, U.S. senators Rufus King of New York and Oliver Ellsworth of Connecticut approached Senator John Taylor of Virginia and urged him to support a move to divide the Union. They informed the astonished Virginian that the differences between the North and South were too profound for ordinary political means to resolve.[5] Only separate countries could do it.

Senator Henry Cabot Lodge of Massachusetts wrote in 1883: "When the Constitution was adopted by the States at Philadelphia, and accepted by the votes of the States in popular conventions, it is safe to say that there was not a man in the country, from Washington and Hamilton on one side to George Clinton and George Mason on the other, who regarded the new system as anything but an experiment entered upon by the States, and from which each and every State had the right peacefully to withdraw, a right which was very likely to be exercised."[6]

There was never a time from 1789 to 1860 when a division of the Union was not publicly discussed. Sometimes the discussions were more serious than others. Ironically, it was New England threatening to leave.

The Northeast discussed seceding over the Louisiana Purchase (1803), Jefferson's embargo against Great Britain and France (1807), and the War of 1812. From December 15, 1814, to January 5, 1815, delegates from the states of Massachusetts, Connecticut, New Hampshire, Vermont, and Rhode Island met to discuss their grievances with Washington and to consider seceding from the Union. They decided against secession for practical reasons—not because they had any Constitutional reservations. No one at that time believed secession was illegal. As historian Shelby Foote remarked, "If they [the states] had known that they couldn't get out, they would never have gotten in."[7]

Thomas Jefferson. *Courtesy of the White House Historical Association;* Alexander Hamilton. *Courtesy of the National Portrait Gallery*

The Northeast openly considered seceding again over the question of the annexation of Texas (1845-1848) and the Fugitive Slave Act (1850). Abolitionist leader William Lloyd Garrison and his minions advocated secession throughout the 1840s and 1850s because they did not want to remain in a Union with slavery in it. In all, New England seriously considered secession five times: 1) over the Louisiana Purchase, 2) over Jefferson's embargo, 3) because of the War of 1812, 4) over the annexation of Texas, and 5) over the Fugitive Slave Act. Except for South Carolina, the South only seriously considered secession twice: after seeing the Northern reaction to the John Brown raid and after the election of Abraham Lincoln in 1860.[8] The difference was that New England just talked about it. The South did it.

After the Civil War, Northern historians assumed that the Union was "indivisible" and illegitimately transported that assumption back to the founding of the country. To them, the South was evil, and secession had always been wrong. The South could not possibly have had a valid reason for seceding, which is the idea these biased historians believed and promoted. But 750,000 dead by 1865, and many more wounded and suffering to the end of their lives, was a high price to pay for stopping secession in the abstract. A morally repugnant reason, therefore, was concocted and assigned to Dixie. Fortunately for Northern historians, the morally abhorrent institution of slavery—of which the North had only recently divested itself, from which it profited until 1885, and which largely funded its industrial revolution—was conveniently available. The fact that there is a vast body of evidence to the contrary and that the Southerners of that time gave several other reasons for secession was, and still is, simply ignored. But this is a highly successful Marxist tactic: focus on something that people find highly repugnant and then build an analytic framework around it.

In 1863, as if to underline its hypocrisy, the United States government recognized the right of West Virginia to secede from Virginia and admitted it to the Union as a separate state—in time to vote for Lincoln in the election of 1864. The U.S. Supreme Court recognized this "right" in 1866. So we see that secession in the first person—"our secession" —is legal. Only in the third person— "their secession"—does it become illegal.

CHAPTER IV

PREGNANT EVENTS

*Governments are like revolutions; you may put them in
motion but I defy you to control them after they are in
motion.*

—John Randolph of Roanoke

Despite significant cultural differences, the American Republic began
its checkered voyage under the Constitution. George Washington
was inaugurated the first president on April 30, 1789, and on July 4, he
signed the Tariff of 1789. It was a revenue tariff, as opposed to a protective tariff, although it did offer some protection for emerging manufacturing industries.[1] The 1789 tariff provided for an 8 percent tax on
imported foreign goods, which placed an undue burden on the South,
whose income, based on agricultural exports, was dependent on foreign
imports.[2]

There was no income tax in the United States before the Civil War,
so tariffs were the primary source of federal revenues. Between 1789 and
1815, the overall tariff rates varied between 6.5 and 15.1 percent depending on funding needs.[3]

Meanwhile, on August 14, 1791, a slave revolt began in Haiti. Within
weeks, 100,000 slaves joined the rebellion. They killed 4,000 whites and
destroyed 180 sugar plantations and 900 coffee plantations, as well as
hundreds of large indigo farms. The revolution was characterized by
extreme violence, torture, rape, and murder. Entire families were wiped

out. Survivors often escaped with only the clothes on their backs. Many of them fled to the American South, carrying their stories of horror with them. Meanwhile, the whites who remained on the island formed militia units, which killed some 15,000 black people in an orgy of revenge. The fighting lasted until 1804, when Haiti became an independent republic under black leadership. It was the only successful slave insurrection in the history of the Western Hemisphere.

The events in Haiti frightened slave owners throughout the United States but especially in the South, where blacks became concentrated after the invention of the Whitney gin made cotton production so popular. To the Southerner, nothing was more serious than servile insurrection. This fact loomed in the background throughout the antebellum period, and anyone considering slavery, race relations, and Caucasian attitudes in the Old South should keep this in mind.

Vice President John Adams of Massachusetts succeeded George Washington as president in 1797. By now, there were two political parties in the United States: the Federalists (led by Hamilton and Adams) and the Republicans, who followed the ideas of Thomas Jefferson. The wealthier and more aristocratic Federalists concentrated in the Northeast and looked down on most Old World immigrants, who were flooding into the country. Consequently, many immigrants supported the more notably inclusive party of Jefferson.

In 1798, the Federalist Congress passed a series of anti-immigration laws called the Alien and Sedition Acts. Among other things, they raised the residency requirements on immigrants from five to fourteen years for citizenship and restricted the speech of people who defamed government officials, including the president. Outlawing criticism of the ruling class was a violation of the First Amendment in spirit, if not the law itself, and opponents challenged the Acts in court; but the Federalist-dominated Supreme Court voted for political expediency and ruled in favor of the government. It was a transparent attempt to silence the opposition. Adams' people indicted dozens of pro-Jefferson newspaper editors and put several on trial, although few were fined or went to jail.

In response, Thomas Jefferson and James Madison secretly wrote the Virginia and Kentucky Resolutions. Their respective legislatures passed them in late 1798. They argued that individual states had the power to declare federal laws unconstitutional, although they did not use the term "nullification." A second Kentucky Resolution (1799) declared that if a state found a law unconstitutional, nullification was the proper remedy. (It did use the term "nullification.") Alexander Hamilton's remedy was entirely different. He wanted Adams to send the army to Virginia to enforce the Acts. Cooler heads prevailed, however.

James Madison. *Courtesy of the White House Historical Association*

The Resolutions put the Federalists on the defensive and likely cost Adams his reelection bid. Jefferson won the presidential election of 1800 by an electoral vote of seventy-three to sixty-five. This triumph was what Dr. Livingston called a "racial trauma" for the New Englanders. Because he slept with a black woman, they considered Jefferson racially tarnished and called him the "first Negro president."[4] They also resented the fact that black folks counted as three-fifths of a person for census purposes, which determined the allocation of electoral votes. If it had not been for this "three-fifths rule," Adams would have been reelected.[5]

Northerners of that day were highly prejudiced against black people, and they kept this bias throughout the Civil War era. In fact, it was at this time that their intellectuals and scientists produced the first theories that black people were subhuman and not of the same species as whites. Josiah C. Nott, a descendant of one of Connecticut's oldest families, and Louis Agassiz, a zoology professor at Harvard, were two of the most respected scientists of their day. They argued that blacks and whites were not of the same species, that black people were racially inferior to whites, and that whites were not related to blacks, in the same way that whites were not related to monkeys. Nott described his racial theories as "niggerology."[6]

It was widely believed in the North that the black population in North America would eventually die out if they were ever freed. New England's most popular and respected writer, Ralph Waldo Emerson, commented that the black was "destined for the museums, like the Dodo." It shocked Jefferson Davis the first time he heard Northern senators talking about the extinction of the African-American race as a matter of course.[7]

Thomas Jefferson once suggested that the slaves could go to the Western lands and find liberation. He received no support from the North, but Virginia statesman John Randolph thought it was a capital idea.[8] He freed his 518 slaves in his will and caused them to be sent to Ohio, to lands they inherited from him, along with supplies provided by his estate. But Ohio refused to accept them.[9] The free black contingent had to return to Virginia and ask to be made wards of the state.

In 1816, during the "Era of Good Feeling," when partisan political rancor was low, Secretary of the Treasury Alexander J. Dallas sought to pay for the War of 1812 and protect emerging U.S. manufacturing industries from European competition by increasing tariffs from 6.5 to 20.2 percent. Southern congressmen and even some Federalists strongly opposed the bill, but it passed the House eighty-eight to fifty-four. It was, however, only a temporary measure, set to expire in June 1820. The legislation also created a Second Bank of the United States.[10]

Historian Norris W. Preyer later wrote that the Southern leadership, including Calhoun, Madison, and Jefferson, supported the Tariff of 1816 because of prosperity, patriotism, and promises that it would not be permanent.[11] National prosperity, however, ended with the financial Panic of 1819. By this time, the Era of Good Feelings had passed, and Southerners were concerned that continuing the high tariffs would cause the British to retaliate and tax raw cotton. (In 1820, five years after the conclusion of the War of 1812, the British were not particularly happy with their American cousins anyway.) But the Tariff of 1816 had some unintended consequences. First, the North became addicted to protective tariffs—and with incredible speed. Second, the nature of the tariff itself changed. It became a corrupt system for the redistribution of wealth by political means. Third, Northern manufacturers were now able to charge more for their own products and thus reap higher profits because the tariffs (taxes) on imported British goods were so high. On the other hand, Southerners experienced higher production costs and higher cost-of-living expenses because of the tariffs. The Tariff of 1816 began what one historian called "a thirty-year tariff war." It also began a forty-five-year run-up to a war of an entirely different nature.

●●●

In 1819, Missouri applied for statehood. People assumed its admission to the Union would be as a slave state, but there were other issues. Constitutional questions, economic problems, slavery, political divisions, and cultural difference overlapped in a complex mosaic. Representative James Tallmadge Jr., of New York, tossed a political bomb by attaching an accelerated emancipation bill to it. The ensuing explosion blew apart the Era of Good Feeling. Tallmadge had played a leading role in the emancipation of slaves in New York and later campaigned against the restrictive Black Codes in Illinois. Tallmadge's measure tied up Congress for a year.[12]

The deadlock of 1819–1820 was a political one. The North already outnumbered the South one hundred five to eighty-one in the House of Representatives, but the Senate was evenly divided. Missouri then was unquestionably Southern. It had 60,000 inhabitants (including 10,000 slaves), and most of them came from Virginia, North Carolina, and Kentucky. Keeping Missouri out of the Union because of the slavery issue seemed to the South a thin pretext for a cynical Northern power play. Among the leaders of the anti-admission faction was Northern flesh peddler Senator James DeWolff of Rhode Island. DeWolff was one of the wealthiest men in the United States. He made his money in the New England slave trade. His company ran eighty voyages to Africa before Washington shut down the importation of human beings to the U.S.A. in 1808. After that, DeWolff's ships engaged in the global slave trade.[13]

To the Southern leaders, DeWolff's opposition smacked of hypocrisy. They believed his position was merely a reflection of the New England Federalist position—an attempt to limit Southern agrarian political power, which advocated westward expansion and free trade and opposed the national bank and government subsidies to business. (The federal government then subsidized the New England business sector, including fishing and manufacturing interests.)

Henry Clay, the speaker of the House, authored a successful compromise. Missouri joined the Union as a slave state, while Maine (until then part of Massachusetts) joined as a free state. The rest of the Louisiana Purchase was divided along a line that ran parallel with Missouri's southern border. North of the line was free territory; south of it was open to slavery.

The Compromise of 1820 was a political solution to a political issue, and it kept peace between the sections for a while. Meanwhile, the State of Missouri's Constitution went into effect. It prohibited free black people from entering the state. Later, Illinois enacted a similar measure called the "Black Codes." Abraham Lincoln, then a member of the legislature, fully supported the Codes, and he never spoke against them.

Lincoln was also a member of the American Colonization Society, a significant part of the "back to Africa" movement, and was secretary of the Illinois branch for many years. He and his colleagues, who included President James Madison, Chief Justice John Marshall, Alexander Hamilton, Daniel Webster, and Stephen Douglas, had a simple solution to the "Negro problem": return every African American to Africa, including those born in the United States. Lincoln personally introduced a bill in the Illinois legislature to expel all black persons (slave or free) from the state. Typically, he advocated a government solution to the problem. He wanted the federal and state governments to buy all the slaves and then deport them to the "Dark Continent."

Other states passed "anti-Negro" measures like the Illinois Black Codes. The cumulative effect restricted the free black population in the Midwest to 1 percent.[14]

In the meantime, a violent abolitionist and would-be terrorist movement developed in the North. Its leaders included Lysander Spooner of Massachusetts, who proposed establishing a para-military force and infiltrating the South with armed units that would merge with blacks and poor whites to form guerrilla groups in wilderness areas to strike at the "Slaveocracy." William Lloyd Garrison, Wendell Phillips, and others joined Spooner. Well-financed by wealthy New Englanders, the abolitionists flooded the South with handbills calling for slave revolts. This action had a chilling effect on the South, which feared servile insurrection more than anything else. Southerners began to look north with suspicion and increasing distaste.

●●●   ·

Conditions continued to deteriorate in 1824. The dynamic, hard-drinking Henry Clay was a major player in Washington. Although he was a slaveholder, he advocated sending all black people back to Africa, though many of them had never been there. He was the political idol of Abraham Lincoln and, at the time of his death, president of the American Colonialization Society. Clay advocated what he called the "American

System." Rooted in Alexander Hamilton's American School,[15] it was designed to allow the fledgling U.S. manufacturing sector in the North to compete with British manufacturing through the imposition of high tariffs. It also called for high public land prices to generate income for Washington, D.C., and to finance internal improvements (i.e., public works projects, such as roads and canals). Later, it included the subsidizing of railroads. Today, it would be considered corporate welfare. Clay's ideas would also help Northern manufacturing interests by keeping immigrant workers in the cities because they could not afford to buy land for farms. This surplus of workers, of course, meant the factory owners could force their employees to work long hours for low pay, and they were easy to replace if hurt or sick. Some contemporary observers declared that slaves owned by a humane master were better off than free people living in the crowded, unhealthy tenements of the dirty Northern cities.

The American System became Abraham Lincoln's political North Star and was one political position from which he never wavered.

In 1824, Clay, as speaker of the House, proposed a new tariff in which the average rate was about 35 percent. It was obviously protective in nature, and Clay had to strain every political muscle to get it passed. The opposition was fierce. The South's prosperity depended on low-cost imports from Great Britain and open foreign markets for its cotton. It was a high tariff versus free trade showdown. Clay engaged in deal-making, "log rolling," and "horse trading" to swing votes. He was successful. The Tariff of 1824 passed the House one hundred seven to one hundred two, and the Senate twenty-five to twenty-one. The legislatures of South Carolina, Georgia, and North Carolina condemned the act as unconstitutional because it subsidized one branch of the economy (manufacturing) at the expense of commerce and agriculture.[16] John C. Calhoun of South Carolina declared that the government should not tax one section of the economy or one region of the country for the enrichment of another.[17]

Henry Clay, "the Great Compromiser" and Lincoln's political idol. *Courtesy of the Ohio State University*

The Tariff of 1824 was a sign of Northern political dominance in the United States. It was also a sign that Northern hegemony meant economic exploitation and poverty for the South. To Southerners, it proved that Northerners would ignore the Constitution if its economic interests were involved. James Spence wrote: "The idea of a moderate system, generally beneficial to the industry of the country, without grievous hardship to any particular class, became altered into the reality of corrupt political bargains between special interests, to impose heavy taxation on all others for their own profit."[18]

In the meantime, the discredited Federalist party collapsed, and all major presidential candidates in 1824 were members of the Democrat-Republican party. This might suggest that there was national political unity; in fact, nothing could be further from the truth. There were four major candidates: John Quincy Adams of Massachusetts (son of John Adams), General Andrew Jackson of Tennessee, Henry Clay of Kentucky, and Secretary of the Treasury William H. Crawford. The bitterly contested election was thrown into the House of Representatives. In what Jackson supporters labeled a "Corrupt Bargain," Clay threw his support to Adams, who became president. He promptly named Henry Clay secretary of state. Four years later, Andrew Jackson defeated Adams. Jackson's chief lieutenant, "the little magician," Martin Van Buren, replaced Clay.

● ● ●

Another seminal event occurred in St. John the Baptist Parish, Louisiana, in 1811. Five hundred blacks launched a slave rebellion. They marched down the road in military formation, burning homes and killing whites. Militia units from Baton Rouge, troops from New Orleans, and white planters from the west bank of the Mississippi quickly quelled the revolt. They killed at least sixty-six black people and captured sixteen more. They took them to New Orleans and hanged them.[19]

In Southampton County, Virginia, in August 1831, an African American named Nat Turner led another slave revolt. He and his followers killed between fifty-five and sixty-five people, including at least fifty-one whites—many of them women and children. At least one baby was murdered while still in the crib. The Virginia militia quickly crushed the revolt and killed at least one hundred blacks. Many were beheaded and had their heads mounted on poles along what is now State Route 658. The state executed fifty-six more, including Turner himself. Again, shock waves traveled through the South.

Some people, North and South, agreed that the idea of ending slavery was the moral choice, but not if it was carried out by immoral means, such as those Turner employed. Others, including many abolitionists, believed the ends justified the means. Some of them were already calling for violence against all Southerners, not just slave owners. Though the minority, the abolitionist rhetoric became so loud and vile that it made rational discussion impossible. The abolitionists offered only two choices:

1) immediate and uncompensated emancipation or 2) the threat of terrorism.

The South chose to face the second alternative.

• • •

Far too many historians divide white people of the 1820–1860 era into two categories: abolitionists or supporters of the Slaveocracy, but there is a third category: emancipationists.

Abolitionists were irresponsible. Immediate, uncompensated liberation would have resulted in chaos and economic collapse for both the North and the South. But supporters of slavery were going against the flow of history. When Lincoln and others offered them a deal to emancipate their slaves and forcibly transport them to Africa for free to boot, they should have taken them up on it.

The emancipationists were the people in the political center on the slavery issue. Ironically, they included men like Abraham Lincoln and Robert E. Lee. They wanted a gradual, compensated emancipation, but they never answered a number of questions: mainly, how to achieve it, how much should be paid, how to go about it, and what time frame should be involved. Most of them had no idea where to start.

Meanwhile, the North and the state of South Carolina almost came to blows, and it had nothing to do with slavery. It was mostly about money.

CHAPTER V

THE NULLIFICATION CRISIS

*South Carolina will preserve its sovereignty or be buried
beneath it.*

—Senator Robert Young Hayne, 1832

*The real causes of dissatisfaction in the South with the North,
are in the unjust taxation and expenditure of taxes... and in
the revolution the North has effected in this government, from
a confederated republic, to a national sectional despotism.*

—Charleston Mercury *editorial, November 8, 1860*

The question of who could interpret constitutional issues was not addressed in the Constitution. Seeing an opportunity, the federal judiciary quickly tried to usurp this power for itself. Some of the Founders soon realized that, if this continued, the only restraint on the federal government would be the federal government itself, an oxymoron. To stop this development, they asserted that this power accrued to the states under the Tenth Amendment, which clearly states that rights not delegated to the federal government are retained by the states or the people.

The idea of states having power to nullify laws in the United States goes back to colonial days. The British Parliament passed the Stamp Act in 1765, but the North American colonies considered it an illegal tax and resorted to mob violence to resist it. Fearing for their lives, the intimidated tax collectors resigned. This, in effect, nullified the act, which the British Parliament repealed in 1766. They followed it with other attempts at taxation, including the Boston Port Act, the Massachusetts Government Act, the Administration of Justice Act, and the Quartering Act.

Taken together, these are called the Coercive Acts or the Intolerable Acts. Massachusetts led the way in resisting and trying to nullify them, resulting in the Boston Tea Party, the Suffolk Resolves,[1] and the forming of the First Continental Congress. But did the states still have the right to do so after they joined the United States? This question would need an answer.

The first skirmish of this legal war occurred in 1792, when Alexander Chisholm, the executor of the estate of Robert Farquhar, sued the State of Georgia for payments of goods Farquhar delivered to the state during the Revolution. The case was tried in Supreme Court, but the Georgian lawyers refused to appear, claiming that, as a sovereign state, Georgia could not be sued without its permission.

Chisholm won the case four to one with the court ruling that, under Article 3, Section 2, the Constitution abrogated the states' sovereign immunity and gave Federal courts the power to rule on suits between citizens and the states (i.e., federal courts were above the states).

This decision was a significant victory for centralized government because a branch of the federal government had placed itself above a sovereign state. It was a short-lived triumph, however. Congress and the states passed the Eleventh Amendment, which restored the states' sovereign immunity. They also reacted in record time. In 1794–1795, they had no telephones, faxes, internet, or even decent roads. Even so, the opponents of the ruling obtained the required twelve votes to ratify in just eleven months. South Carolina ratified it later. Only New Jersey and Pennsylvania did not act on the amendment.[2] The centralization of federal power by means of the judicial branch had been temporarily checked.

The second major battle on the constitutional issue of who had been right to review or nullify a federal measure centered around the Alien and Sedition Acts. The Democrat-Republicans declared the acts null with the Kentucky and Virginia Resolutions, but this crisis ended without a clear resolution.

Later, after Jefferson won the election of 1800, lame-duck President John Adams tried to pack the federal courts with sixteen Federalist judges, who would have lifetime appointments to the recently created seats on the bench (the Judiciary Act of 1801, also known as the Midnight Judges Act, created these seats). Adams was at his desk until nine in the evening on March 3, 1801, his last day in office, signing judicial appointments.[3] He then fled the city so he would not have to attend Thomas's Jefferson's inauguration.

Jefferson's inaugural address was a thing of toleration, art, and beauty. New England was once again threatening to leave the Union because it had lost the election. Jefferson invited it to do so. "If there be any among us who would wish to dissolve the Union," he said, "or to change its republican form, let them stand undisturbed as monuments of the safety with which error of opinion may be tolerated where reason is left free to combat it." Nevertheless, Jefferson and his supporters in Congress were not about to let the "Midnight Judges Act" stand. The new Congress repealed the Judicial Act, and Jefferson swept the lower court benches clear.[4] But Adams' appointee as Chief Justice of the Supreme Court, John Marshall, could not be swept away so easily. Marshall, who was Jefferson's cousin, cleverly inserted the principle of judicial review into the decision on the landmark case of *Marbury v. Madison* (1803). The ball was now in Jefferson's court. He had to accept the concept of judicial review or attack the court.

Jefferson attacked the court. His target was Samuel Chase, a particularly arrogant and obnoxious Federalist supreme court judge, who delivered offensive anti-Republican harangues from the bench. Led by John Randolph of Roanoke, the House impeached him in 1804, and the case went to the Senate for trial. The Constitution, however, required that a justice commit "high crimes and misdemeanors" before he could be impeached. Being obnoxious, politically biased, and unfair are not crimes listed in the Constitution, so Chase was acquitted. The Supreme Court was thus able to create for itself the right of judicial review, even though it was not in the Constitution.

At this point, the issue of who else, besides the Supreme Court, had the right of constitutional review was still undecided.

• • •

Meanwhile, in the early 1830s, the South inched toward emancipation.

In the 1830s, there were more anti-slavery societies in the South than the North. The 106 Southern anti-slavery societies had 5,150 members. The twenty-four anti-slavery organizations in the North had 1,475 members.[5]

In 1832, after the Nat Turner Massacre, Virginia governor John Floyd called a special session of the legislature to consider the question of emancipation. Every argument concerning slavery, pro and con, was debated. For a time, it appeared that the emancipationists would carry the day, but in the end, the special session affirmed slavery by a small majority, sixty-five to fifty-eight.[6] The emancipationists only lost because they could not agree on the details. The delegates did pass a resolution seventy-three to fifty-eight that admitted slavery was evil.[7] This resolution suggests that there was a considerable amount of support for emancipation. Although disappointed with the results, supporters found the strength of their support encouraging. The anti-slavery forces in Virginia looked forward to the future when they believed they would succeed in abolishing the "peculiar institution" in the Old Dominion.

At this point, Dr. Livingston records, the Northeastern abolitionists "began their theatrical antics demanding immediate, uncompensated emancipation, backed by threats of terror and Northern secession."[8] The Southerners did not like people coming down and telling them how to live. As a result, the slavery issue became sectional. By 1850, there were zero anti-slave societies in the South.[9]

• • •

Henry Clay's Missouri Compromise quieted the slave question for twenty-five years, but it did nothing about growing sectionalism.

America teetered on the brink of civil war in 1833 over an issue that had nothing to do with human bondage. The country almost came to blows over tariffs and the issue of nullification and states' rights.

South Carolina had already successfully nullified a Federal action. In 1822, Denmark Vesey, a free black minister in Charleston and one of the founders of the African Methodist Episcopal Church (AME), was angry because he had been unable to buy his first wife and children out of slavery. He became the ringleader of a planned slave rebellion in which he plotted to kill the slave owners of Charleston and the surrounding area. He and his followers would then sail to Haiti. Unfortunately for Vesey, city officials found out about it and suppressed the revolt before it was launched. Found guilty, Vesey and some thirty-five of his followers were hanged; others were deported. The Charlestonians destroyed his church.[10]

The South Carolina planters believed that free black sailors from British ships had conspired with Vesey in his slave revolt. The South Carolina legislature quickly passed the Negro Seaman Act, which required the confinement of all foreign black sailors to their ships while they were docked in South Carolina ports. If a black sailor disobeyed the law and came ashore, he faced arrest and the prospect of enslavement. London strongly objected, mainly because its captains were trying to recruit more African-American and African sailors. The other Southern states—which also feared servile insurrection—quickly replicated South Carolina's actions. The entire matter soon ended up in court.

In those days, Supreme Court justices doubled as circuit judges. Justice William Johnson, in his role as a circuit judge, declared the Negro Seamen Act unconstitutional because it violated U.S. treaties with the United Kingdom. Johnson may have been legally correct, but that did not matter. The South Carolina Senate nullified the judge's ruling. The Negro Seaman Act was enforced, and the federal government under President James Monroe made no attempts to enforce Judge Johnson's decree.

In the last years of his life, Jefferson recommended that Virginia reassert her sovereignty and nullify federal internal improvement legislation, which he considered unconstitutional.[11] He also reflected on slavery. "As it is," he wrote, "we have the wolf by the ears, and we can neither hold him, nor safely let him go."[12]

Jefferson died in 1826. Two years later, led by Henry Clay, a new tariff passed the House one hundred five to ninety-four and the Senate twenty-six to twenty-one. It was a huge tax increase. Rates skyrocketed to an average of about 47 percent, and to 51 percent on implements with iron in them. Southern representatives in the House voted against it fifty to three. There were howls of protest throughout Dixie, which labeled it the "Tariff of Abominations."

The Constitution allowed a tariff for revenue purposes. For those who interpreted the document strictly, this did not mean that it authorized a tariff to protect domestic manufacturers from foreign competition or to favor one section of the country over another. The South solidly opposed protective tariffs, correctly envisioning that restraints on free trade would mean economic exploitation of an exporting region like the Cotton States.

The Tariff of 1828 resulted in John Quincy Adams losing the presidential race to Jackson that same year. Andrew Jackson was a hot-tempered, intolerant military man and slaveholder. He was a strict constructionist, and, although he sympathized with South Carolina about the tariff, he was a pragmatist who did not believe it should be replaced until the national debt was paid off. (Most of the debt was caused by over expenditures on internal improvements in the North. "Internal improvements" in today's terms means government subsidies to private industry, corporate welfare and crony capitalism, and catering to special interest groups. In the nineteenth century, they were characterized by corruption and enthusiastically supported by Abraham Lincoln and other Northern Whigs.) Despite his sympathy for the South, Jackson would not sanction nullification or secession.

The Senate debate of 1830 was largely between Daniel Webster of Massachusetts and his allies on one side, and Robert Y. Hayne of South Carolina, Thomas Hart Benton, and their allies on the other. According to establishment historical mythology, the intellectually outstanding Webster, using his vastly superior debating skills, isolated the South, discredited states' rights, nullification, secession, and strict constructionism, and affirmed the principles of implied powers, strong central government, federal supremacy, and an indivisible, perpetual Union— all by himself and in only a couple of speeches. H. A. Scott Trask, writing in 2016, convincingly shattered this myth.[13] Trask examined the documents and newspapers of that time, which give an entirely different picture. At least as people many believed Hayne had defeated Webster.

Left: Robert Young Hayne. *Courtesy of J. B. Longaere;* Right: Daniel Webster, who appears to have been weaned on a pickle. *Courtesy of Matthew Brady*

The debate began on December 29, 1829, when Senator Samuel A. Foot of Connecticut introduced a resolution of inquiry as to whether it would be desirable to limit the sale of public lands indefinitely and to stop the survey of new areas. The next day, Senator Benton of Missouri rose and denounced the proposal as just another attempt by New England to stop immigration to the western states. Their hidden aim, he declared, was to keep people in the East to work in their factories. On January 18, 1830, he spoke again and charged that the business classes of the East were trying to enrich themselves by taxing the South, injuring the West, and pauperizing the poor of the North.

The next day, Senator Hayne gave a short oration calling for a lower tariff and a reduction in the price of public lands sold to settlers in the West. He pointed out that, under current policies, only the East benefited.

Webster spoke on January 20. He rebutted Hayne, attacked the South and its institutions, and declared that Southerners were hurting the country by opposing the growing power of the central government. He did not mention Benton or the West. But Benton rose and mentioned him that day. He correctly accused Webster of trying to isolate the South and form an alliance between the North and West, creating a coalition like the one that led to the election of Adams in 1824. Benton also alluded to the fact that New England had threatened to secede on more than one occasion and that the region's attitude toward the Union was one of calculated indifference. He added that the West was not fooled. It knew that the South, not New England, had long been its protector.[14]

Hayne spoke again on January 21, attacking the New England faction as motivated by base self-interest and defending his state's right to sovereignty and nullification. He quoted Jefferson's contention that the national government was not the "exclusive or final judge of the extent of its own powers."[15] (Like Marshall, Webster believed the Supreme Court was the exclusive evaluator of constitutional disputes.)

Webster's next speech consumed January 22 and 23. He argued that the Constitution was not a social compact but a permanent, inseparable union.

At this time, the Jacksonian movement had majority support of the American people, who believed Hayne had gotten the better of the argument. In pro-Jackson Maine, for example, the legislature ordered the publication and distribution of 2,000 pamphlets of Hayne's speech and sent him a letter thanking him for defending democracy in New England.

The Webster-Hayne debate continued for months as allies of one faction or the other rose to give their views. Meanwhile, the crisis surroundig the Tariff of 1828 deepened. The South Carolina legislature denounced the tariff as unconstitutional. Behind the scenes, Vice President John C. Calhoun secretly wrote *The South Carolina Exposition and Protest,* which advanced the idea of nullification vis-à-vis the tariff. He asserted that the Tariff of 1828 was unconstitutional because it favored manufacturing over commerce and agriculture. In *Exposition and Protest,* Calhoun held that state conventions (which had originally ratified the Constitution) could nullify any law they considered unconstitutional. The nullification could only be overridden by a three-fourths vote of all the states.

Calhoun intended for nullification to be a moderate compromise between yielding to an outrageously high tariff and secession. Jackson, on the other hand, insisted that all the taxes be collected at once. He demanded immediate and unconditional obedience. South Carolina refused to do this for constitutional and economic reasons. Its economic fortunes were at a low ebb since the Panic of 1819, and, due to Western migration, its population had dropped from 580,000 to just under 500,000 in the 1820s. Many of its planters and yeoman farmers could not afford new taxes. South Carolina congressman George McDuffie, a Calhoun supporter and a very capable speaker, expounded the Forty Bale Theory. The theory declared that the 40 percent tax on finished cotton goods in the Tariff of 1816 meant that "the manufacturer actually invades your barns and plunders you of forty out of every hundred bales that you produce."[16] His message struck home and opened the eyes of many South Carolinians. It made converts to the idea of nullification and stoked the fires of many who already felt the federal government was taking advantage of them.

John C. Calhoun in 1822, at age forty. *Courtesy of Charles Bird King*

Because of the Webster-Hayne debate, Jackson's intransigence, and South Carolina's hardening attitude, Washington featured an overheated political atmosphere in 1830. Even so, social life continued in the nation's capital. Working through Senator Benton, President Jackson arranged an elaborate dinner at the India Queen Hotel on April 13, 1830, to celebrate Thomas Jefferson's birthday. All the important Democrats were there, including Vice President John C. Calhoun.

Senator Hayne was the speaker that evening. He denounced the tariff but avoided any mention of nullification. Then came the voluntary toasts, which were so anti-tariff in nature that some of the guests walked out, including the entire Pennsylvania delegation. Tensions were already high when the special toasts began. President Jackson arose, glass in hand. He did not look at the rest of the audience but pointedly focused his glare solely on John C. Calhoun. "Our Union, it must be preserved," he snapped.

Left: Andrew Jackson, c. 1837. *Courtesy of the White House Historical Association;*
Right: John C. Calhoun, 1849, shortly before his death. *Courtesy of Matthew Brady*

The entire room went silent. It could not have been more dramatic had Jackson ordered federal officers to arrest Calhoun on the spot. The vice president was scheduled to give the next toast. He arose, looked directly at Jackson, and in a firm voice said: "The Union, next to our liberty, most dear. May we all remember that it can only be preserved by respecting the rights of the states and by distributing equally the benefits and burdens of the Union."

There were three major implications in this brief toast. First, unity does not outweigh justice and liberty. Second, if unity is not beneficial, it is of no value. Third, tyranny cannot coerce unity by threatening to use bayonets.[17]

By now, many Northern leaders, including Henry Clay, realized that they had gone too far with the Tariff of Abominations. It was assumed, because of the political pressure, that a new tariff would be enacted, lowering the rates significantly, so South Carolina did not take decisive action.

The Tariff of 1832 did indeed lower the rates but not enough. The average tariff for dutiable goods was 33 percent. Thanks to the tariffs, about 90 percent of which were paid by Southerners, the United States now had a budget surplus, but the Northerners drafted a bill that kept the tariffs high and protected the manufacturers' profit margins at the expense of the South. Many Southerners felt hoodwinked. Much of the rest of Dixie wanted a better compromise, but South Carolina was ready to act. Governor James Hamilton[18] conducted pro-nullification, anti-tariff rallies throughout the state. As a result, the nullification forces won the state election of 1832 by a large majority.

On October 20, 1832, South Carolina Governor Hamilton called for a special session to authorize a nullification convention. The legislature concurred, and the convention met on November 24. It chose Senator Hayne presiding officer and quickly declared the Tariffs of 1828 and 1832 unconstitutional and nullified them. State and federal officials were forbidden from collecting tariffs within the state after February 1, 1833. The leadership vowed to secede if the United States government tried coercion. Jackson, meanwhile, could not tolerate opposition, and it was leaked that Calhoun was the author of *Exposition and Protest*. Jackson was privately threatening to lead an invasion of the Palmetto State and hang Calhoun from the nearest tree. Publicly, Old Hickory declared that he would use force to prevent nullification.

Meanwhile, Hamilton's term as governor was expiring, and the South Carolina legislature picked Hayne to succeed him. He resigned from the Senate on December 13, and the assembly elected John C. Calhoun to replace him. Knowing his alliance with Jackson was forever shattered, Calhoun resigned as vice president on December 28 to take his Senate seat.[19]

On January 16, 1833, Jackson requested Congress pass the Force Bill authorizing military intervention in South Carolina. The state mobilized 27,000 men. Washington and Charleston were plainly on a collision course.

The end of the nullification crisis was anti-climactic. The Force Bill and South Carolina mobilization frightened Henry Clay and Jackson's chief lieutenant, Martin Van Buren. Both had supported the Tariff of Abominations, but both wanted to avoid war, as did a great many others. Clay met privately with Calhoun, and the two worked out a compromise. It did not please everyone, but it satisfied enough.

South Carolina did not want to fight the United States, either. It postponed the enforcement of nullification and thus took a giant step back from war, while its agents in Washington, D.C., worked things out.

Left: Governor James Hamilton Jr. of South Carolina. *Courtesy of the South Carolina Encyclopedia;* Right: Martin Van Buren, President Jackson's chief lieutenant and eighth president of the United States. *Courtesy of the Brady-Hanley Collection, Library of Congress*

Few people wanted to go to war over taxes, so the Tariff of 1833 (the Clay-Calhoun agreement) passed the House one hundred nineteen to eighty-five and the Senate twenty-nine to sixteen. It gradually rolled back the tariffs over a nine-year period until 1842, when it reached the levels of the 1816 Tariffs—about 20 percent.

Now that the danger of war had passed, everybody breathed a sigh of relief. South Carolina, however, made one final gesture of defiance. It nullified the Force Act.

● ● ●

The question of nullification is still with us today. California, for example, is trying to nullify federal immigration laws. It is also talking secession. Parts of California are talking about seceding from other parts of California. There is also a serious secession movement in Hawaii, and strong elements in eastern Washington would like to secede from the extremely liberal state government in Olympia. It will be interesting to see how events play out out on America's left coast.

CHAPTER VI

CULTURAL DIFFERENCES

We are not fighting for slavery.
We are fighting for independence.
—*Jefferson Davis, 1864*

The South has always had a different culture than the North. It was (is) more leisurely and less money-oriented. Yankee culture was more labor intensive, hurried, and placed a higher value on economic profit. Anthony Trollope, a British citizen who traveled extensively in both regions, wrote in 1861: "The South is seceding from the North because the two are not homogeneous. They have different instincts, different appetites, different morals, and a different culture."[1]

Trollope continued: "They [Southerners] had become a separate people, dissevered from the North by habits, morals, institutions, pursuits, and every conceivable difference in their modes of thought and action. They still spoke the same language, as do Austria and Prussia; but beyond that tie of language they had no bond but that of a meager political union … "[2]

Even the language was (is) different. George Bernard Shaw once commented that the British and Americans were two people separated by a common language. The same applied (and applies) to the Southerner and the Northerner—not just in accent and pronunciation, but also regarding words, idioms, usage, and style.

John Adams would have agreed. While attending the Continental Congress, he noted the cultural differences between Northerners and Southerners and wrote his wife that the political union between the two people would not hold "without the utmost caution on both sides."[3]

The Southern and Northern populations were different from the start due to their different immigration patterns. The Southerners came mostly from Northern England and Scotland, Northern Ireland, and the Saxon areas of England. The New Englanders came mostly from the traditionally English regions and East Anglia (the Puritans). Some of the people of the Middle Colonies (Quakers) came from the Northern Midlands of England.[4] The cultural differences were there from the beginning, but they intensified as time marched on.

New England, with its Puritan legacy, developed a self-absorbed, holier-than-thou culture that looked down on the rest of America. Their elite believed high tariffs were their natural right, making New England stronger that the rest of the country.[5] They also viewed nature as something dark and foreboding, an evil to be conquered and controlled. The Southerner saw nature as something to embrace and enjoy. They loved hunting, fishing (usually with a cane pole), and horse racing (gambling), and had a relaxed attitude toward life and nature. Some even saw the South as close to paradise on earth.

Cultures, of course, change over time. From the 1790s on, there was a decline in orthodox Christianity in the Northeast but not in the South. Although they did have their "great awakenings," Unitarianism and other intellectual movements which originated in Europe, German philosophy, and the French Revolution gradually replaced the strict Calvinism of New England. Ralph Waldo Emerson, for example, went to Germany to study. When he returned, he resigned from the Congregational clergy and rejected its sacraments. "Whatever is old corrupts," he declared.[6]

By 1850, the North had many secular humanists, including atheists, deists, transcendentalists, and assorted other non-believers. Many of them had a philosophy that advocated human, rather than religious, values. They looked only to man, science, and government for solutions to their problems.

The South, on the other hand, embraced religion. Through prayer, it looked to God for guidance and regarded secular humanism with suspicion and often with outright hostility. Baptist churches and Churches of Christ sprang up all over the place. Unpretentious, fervent country preachers expounded their simple truths straight from the Bible and gained thousands of converts, and their tent revivals became famous. Even today, the South is known as the Bible Belt. The fact that many Northerners use the term derogatorily while many Southerners (including this author) consider it a compliment further illustrates the differences between the two cultures.

In important ways, however, the "elites" of New England stayed the same. They intermarried and had a strong regional identity. They considered themselves the only real Americans and looked down on Southerners, with their French, Spanish, American Indian, and even African cultural influences, and certainly they considered themselves vastly superior to the uncouth Westerners. They especially looked down on Southerners because of the integrated nature of Southern society. Alexis de Tocqueville wrote: "Race prejudice seems stronger in those states that have abolished slavery than in those where it still exists, and nowhere is it more intolerant than in those states where slavery was never known."[7]

Abraham Lincoln might have agreed. Certainly, he looked down on black people and favored segregation. "What I would most desire would be the separation of the white and black races," he said.[8]

Segregation, as embraced by Lincoln, was possible in the North but not in the South. Contrary to the way Hollywood movies often portray them, most slave owners had a conscience. Most of them felt it was their duty to see to it that their slaves had the opportunity to become Christians. The servants attended church with their masters, listened to the same sermons, lived on the same property, traveled in the same wagons and carriages, and sometimes lived in the same houses. Black women often served as wet nurses for white babies, something Northerners found offensive, if not odious.

Only in the South did the black population continue to grow after the slave trade ended, one indication of relatively good treatment. In the other areas, there was no natural increase. The sugar plantations of the Caribbean and other regions required continuous importation of slaves.[9] Union general Carl Schurz, a radical socialist and a Republican, was sent to investigate conditions in the South after the war, including the newly freed slaves. He was astonished to learn that "centuries of slavery have not been sufficient to make them enemies of the white man."[10]

The reader who is deeply interested in this topic should look up "Slave Narratives" on the internet. In the 1930s, historians interviewed hundreds of ex-slaves as part of the Federal Writers' Project. The African-Americans made it clear that they hated slavery, but the federal writers found that, in general, these former slaves did not hate white people or even their former masters. There were exceptions, of course, and if one looks hard enough in the *Narratives*, one will find bad masters and cruel ones, but they seem to be the exception rather than the rule. One should keep in mind, however, that when the interviews took place during the Great Depression, these people were old and likely unable to work, and there was no social safety net in the 1930s. Some of them no doubt went hungry and looked back nostalgically on the days of their youth. Say what you will about "Massa"—when he was around, everyone on the plantation had enough to eat, out of economic self-interest and Christian charity.[11]

Segregation was a feature of the New South after the antebellum South had been destroyed and "reconstructed" by the North and New England, which demanded racial segregation. The surviving Old Guard from the South opposed segregation because they associated it with the ills of Northern industrial society, as pointed out by C. Vann Woodward in his classic *The Strange Career of Jim Crow*, a book Martin Luther King called "the historical Bible of the civil rights movement."[12]

Northern bigotry and segregation materially contributed to the growing poverty of free blacks. The biographers of abolitionist leader

William Lloyd Garrison wrote: "The free colored people [of New England] were looked upon as an inferior caste to whom their liberty was a curse, and their lot worse than that of the slaves...."[13]

Lincoln's Illinois, for example, had a statute dated 1833 that said blacks could not vote, sit on juries, testify against white people, or attend public schools. If three or more free blacks assembled for the purpose of dancing, they were fined twenty dollars ($540.90 in 2018 dollars[14]) and were to be publicly whipped. They were not to receive more than thirty-nine lashes, however.[15]

Illinois' attitude had not changed twenty years later. In 1853, it passed a law "to prevent the immigration of free negroes into the state." It declared it a misdemeanor for a "Negro or mulatto," slave or free, to come into the state with the intention of living. Another section of the law provided that any black coming into the state in violation of this act faced a fine or temporary slavery to pay for these fines and other costs.[16]

In 1862, the Illinois Constitutional Convention offered a new Constitution, which had the support of President Abraham Lincoln. Article XVIII, Section 1 read: "No negro or mulatto shall immigrate or settle in the state after the adoption of the Constitution." The article was presented for a vote of the people separate from the Constitution. The Constitution was rejected by more than 16,000 votes, but Article XVIII passed by a majority of 100,500 votes and became an organic law in the Illinois Constitution.[17]

Next door, Indiana had similar provisions. In 1851, Article XIII, Section 1 of the new Constitution said: "... no negro or mulatto shall come into or settle in the state after the adoption of this constitution." The clause was adopted by more than 90,000 votes.[18]

As the Northerners moved west and helped populate new states, they carried their attitudes with them. Oregon's 1857 Constitution stated that "No free negro or mulatto, not residing in this state at the time of adoption [of this Constitution] ... shall come, reside, or be within the state."[19] It also provided for the punishment of persons who brought people of color into the state, harbored them, or employed them. The measure was ratified by a popular vote of 8,040 to 1,081.[20]

Nor were these the only states to forbid black people and mulattos from entering. Michigan, Wisconsin, Iowa, Minnesota, California, Colorado, and New Mexico, had similar language in their constitutions. Eugene Berwanger did an in-depth study of racial attitudes in the Northwest (as people called the Midwest in those days) and determined that 79.5 percent of the people of Illinois, Indiana, Oregon, and Kansas voted to exclude free Negroes from their borders "simply because of their prejudice."[21]

John Sherman, the brother of General William T. Sherman, spoke for most of the North when he wrote the general on April 2, 1862: "We do not like the negroes. We do not disguise our dislike. As my friend from Indiana said yesterday: 'The whole people of the Northwestern States are opposed to having many negroes among them and that principle or prejudice has been engraved in the legislation for nearly all the Northwestern States.'"[22]

General Sherman despised the South and hated secession, but he had no problem with slavery. When he was president of the Louisiana Military Academy in Alexandria, he owned at least two domestic servants or "house slaves." He wrote: "All the Congresses on earth can't make the negro anything else than what he is; he must be subject to the white man, or he must amalgamate or be destroyed. Two such races cannot live in harmony, save as master and slave."[23]

The abolitionists believed that slavery was wrong, but they shared the racist attitudes of most Northerners and did not want to associate with black people. Republican Senator Benjamin Wade of Ohio, for example, was a leader in the abolitionist movement and a political ally of Abraham Lincoln but became extremely critical of him when he failed to recruit black soldiers into the Union Army quickly. Privately, he called Lincoln "poor white trash." Wade was as a matter of record intensely bigoted against people of color; during the Civil War, he wanted to send dispensable African-American troops into combat as rapidly as possible so Confederates could kill them instead of white soldiers. In 1851, he called Washington, D.C., "a God-forsaken N**ger ridden place." He wanted to hire a white woman as a housekeeper because "I am sick and tired of n**gers." He complained that he had eaten food cooked "by n**gers until I can smell and taste the n**ger."[24]

Given the hatred much of New England and the rest of the North felt toward people of color, it is absurd and hypocritical to claim that many in the North invaded the South and sacrificed young white men to emancipate slaves.

• • •

Before the Civil War, unlike the industrial North, the South as a whole preferred a prosperous and innovative agricultural way of life because it was profitable and more congenial. The McCormack Reaper, for example, was invented by a Southerner; Edmund Ruffin of Virginia was a pioneer in scientific agriculture, especially in the area of soil rejuvenation; Dr. Rush Nutt of Rodney, Mississippi, developed a branch of cotton that was resistant to rot, as well as an improved cotton gin; and others were prominent in the fields of plant genetics and crop rotation. Innovation was even more noticeable during the Civil War, when a Southerner invented the Gatling gun,[25] Texas Rangers designed the Colt revolver, and Brigadier General Gabriel Rains developed the landmine. Other Southern innovations included ironclads, submarines, electronically detonated mines, and a workable machine gun.[26]

(In 1861, Confederate Captain R. S. Williams of Covington, Kentucky, invented the first machine gun used in combat. Manufactured by the Tredegar Iron Works of Richmond, Virginia, it was a one-pounder steel breech-loader with a four-foot-long barrel and a two-inch bore. It was mounted on a two-wheel carriage and operated by a level attached to a revolving cam, above which was an ammunition hopper. It had a range of 2,000 yards. The South lacked the resources to put it into serial production, but Pickett's Brigade used the prototype most effectively in the Battle of Seven Pines on May 31, 1862. Its Northern opponents were impressed. Later, after the Battle of Gettysburg, several Union officers who had been at Seven Pines approached some of Pickett's officers, who were now prisoners of war, and wanted to know exactly what that marvelous and terrible weapon was.)[27]

Most remarkably, one Southerner, William C. Powers, an architectural engineer in Mobile, Alabama, designed a helicopter in 1862 and even constructed an experimental model, although there is no record of its flying. But there can be no doubt that Powers was ahead of his time. His lattice approach resembled the design later used in the British Vickers Wellington bomber.[28]

Prototype of the Confederate helicopter designed by William C. Powers. *Courtesy of the National Air and Space Museum*

It is popular in the modern media to portray Southerners—antebellum and after—as illiterate. Frank L. Owsley, however, revealed that the literacy rate of the Old South was 91.73 percent. While that was less than that of New England (98.2 percent) and the Northwest (95 percent),[29] it was higher than the male population of Great Britain (75.4 percent), and no one ever refers to the British of that day as uneducated and illiterate. The Old South's white literacy rate, in fact, was higher than every country in Europe except Sweden and Denmark.[30]

The South in 1860 was also more prosperous than either the West, the North, or New England. Of the top eleven states in per capita income, six were Southern. Mississippi was number one and Louisiana was number two.[31] Half the millionaires in the United States lived in the New Orleans-Natchez axis, and one-third of all American millionaires lived in or near Natchez, Mississippi.[32] Nor were all the prosperous people in the Old South planters and plantation owners. There was a significant class of sturdy, yeoman farmers. As the Union army discovered, they also made surprisingly good combat infantrymen.

It is worth reiterating that the South had a severe distaste for people from other regions coming to Dixie and telling them how to live. In New York City in 1860, women and children were working sixteen-hour days on starvation wages. There were more than 150,000 unemployed, 40,000 homeless, 600 brothels (some with girls as young as ten), and 9,000 bars or grog shops. Half of the children of the city did not live past the age of five. Other Northern slums were at least as bad. There were also incredibly wealthy people in the Northern cities who lived in great luxury. Some of them notoriously used dollar bills to light their cigars. Many of the Southern planters or their sons had seen the slums of New York and the slums of London and wanted nothing to do with them. They were not inclined to let upper crust New Yorkers or New Englanders instruct them how to conduct their lives or to allow "those people" to destroy a way of life about which they knew nothing.[33]

One British woman traveling through America just before the war wrote: "The South is seceding from the North because the two are not homogenous. They have different instincts, different appetites, different morals, and a different culture."[34]

In short, long before secession, the North and South had already separated culturally. The North, beginning in New England, had a holier-than-thou attitude born of moral self-deception which unfortunately has become a permanent characteristic of some of their "elites."

CHAPTER VII

AGITATION AND COMPROMISE

The root evil is that the government is engaged in activities in which it has no legitimate business.

—*Barry Goldwater*

William Lloyd Garrison was the son of an alcoholic sailor who abandoned his family. He grew into a staunch Baptist and a vitriolic, harsh, hateful man—an odd combination for a Christian. He became a printer's apprentice and, in 1831, bought *The Liberator*. It became the house organ of the abolitionist movement. The newspaper demanded immediate, uncompensated emancipation, as well as full political rights for all black people. Garrison denounced the Constitution as a covenant with the devil. He and his minions were so fanatical that they refused even to vote.

Garrison looked to shame the slave owners into repentance; failing that, he called upon the North to secede. He also cheered Nat Turner's revolt, which he called the "first step of the earthquake." The suppression of the revolt he called: "A dastardly triumph, well becoming a nation of oppressors."[1]

Left: Frederick Douglass. *Courtesy of the National Archives;* Right: William Lloyd Garrison. *Courtesy of Albert Sands Southworth*

In 1833, Garrison and Arthur Tappen organized the American Anti-Slavery Society.[2] Escaped slave Frederick Douglass, a good speaker and a fine writer, became a key leader. Abolitionists were a small minority at first, but they were extremely vocal. Their positions were not always popular, even in the North. In 1834, a New York City mob sacked Tappen's home, threw his furniture into the street, and burned it. Garrison himself was almost tarred and feathered in Boston in 1835 and was only saved by police, who took him into protective custody. Nevertheless, agitation worked, and the society had 2,000 local chapters and 200,000 members by 1840.[3]

The abolitionists' extreme rhetoric had a polarizing effect, in both North and South, which developed with remarkable speed. Virginia—which narrowly defeated a law abolishing slavery within the state only three years before—enacted a law in 1836 making it a crime to advocate abolition. The Georgia legislature offered a $5,000 reward for anyone who would kidnap Garrison and bring him south to stand trial.[4] In 1838, John C. Calhoun announced that most Southerners—provoked by abolitionist propaganda—had changed their attitude toward slavery. "This agitation has produced one happy effect at least," he declared. "Many in the South once believed that it [slavery] was a moral and political evil;

that folly and delusion are gone; we see it now in its true light, and regard it as the most safe and stable basis for free institutions in the world."[5]

There is no doubt that the extreme abolitionist propaganda had exactly the reverse of its intended effect on the South. Compare Calhoun's remarks to those of Southern leaders just a generation earlier. Thomas Jefferson denounced slavery in 1776 (and repeatedly thereafter) and resolved to free his slaves but was trapped in the system. He could not afford to release his chattels without destroying his personal finances, which were never sound. He did not emancipate his slaves until he was on his deathbed in 1826. He was not alone. George Washington, for example, said, "It is among my first wishes to see some plan adopted by which slavery may be abolished by law." James Madison, the "father of the Constitution," was also a slaveholder, but he said, "It is wrong to admit into the Constitution the idea of property in man."[6]

But, as Reverend Nehemiah Adams of Massachusetts noted, "A great change very soon came over the South." This change, Adams recalled, was the direct result of the propaganda of abolitionist societies. "Publications were scattered through the South whose direct tendency was to stir up insurrection among the colored people." Even found in the blue-paper wrappers of chocolate candies, they were extremely suggestive. "When these amalgamation pictures were discovered," Adams recalled, "husbands and fathers at the South considered that whatever might be true of slavery as a system, self-defence, the protection of their households against a servile insurrection, was their first duty. Who can wonder that they broke into the post-office, and seized and burned abolition papers; indeed, no excesses are surprising, in view of the perils to which they saw themselves exposed."[7]

Prior to the rise of the hysterical abolitionist media, the South was drifting toward gradual emancipation. "We are afraid of your abolitionists," one woman frankly declared.[8] Faced with Northern interference, Southern sentiment reversed itself and embraced slavery. Not content merely to defend themselves, Southerners also attacked Northern society for "wage slavery," and with considerable justification. The distance between the two sides began to get longer. In 1850, near the end of his life, Daniel Webster lamented that the debates leading up to the Compromise of 1850 would have led to the South gradually eliminating slavery had it not been for the frenzy stirred up by the abolitionists.[9]

Emancipation, meanwhile, gained ground worldwide. In 1833, British abolitionists persuaded Parliament to liberate all the slaves in the Empire, including the West Indies colonies. The owners were compensated. France and Denmark followed Britain's lead in 1844, and by 1850, slavery in the Western Hemisphere existed only in the United States, Puerto Rico, Cuba, Brazil, and a few smaller enclaves.

Meanwhile, in 1836, the Republic of Texas applied to join the Union. Most of its people were from the South, and its admission to the Union would add two more Southerners to the Senate and upset the balance of power there. President Jackson refused even to consider it until his hand-picked successor, Martin Van Buren, was elected president. Old Hickory waited until his last day in office even to grant diplomatic recognition to the Texas Republic.

President Van Buren of New York continued to snub Texas, but the Financial Panic of 1837 wrecked his presidency and doomed his reelection bid. In 1840, a Whig was elected president, William Henry Harrison, but he died on April 4, 1841, after only one month in office. He was succeeded by John Tyler of Virginia.

The Whig Party, which had been formed in 1834 in opposition to "King Andrew" Jackson, had two wings: a Henry Clay-Daniel Webster wing and a wing of disaffected Southerners, who had once supported Jackson. This latter wing was led by John C. Calhoun. The Whigs nominated Tyler as vice president to appeal to these disgruntled former Democrats. They had no idea they were choosing the tenth president of the United States.

The Northern Whigs called Tyler "His Accidency." Unlike them, he was pro-states' rights and a strict constructionist, and he vetoed many of their proposals, which he considered unconstitutional, including the national bank and internal improvements, both of which favored the North at the expense of the South. John Tyler believed strict regard for the Constitution was the only way to avoid a civil war in the future, and he refused to sacrifice his principles on the altar of political expediency for his party, even if it cost him his reelection, which it did. Frustrated by Tyler's continual blocking of their agenda, the Whigs expelled him from the party. "By his vetoes he prevented the establishment of a moneyed monopoly represented in the United States [national] bank and by his close personal surveillance of the different departments of the government abolished all corruption and reduced the national expenditures one-fourth," the Richmond *Times-Dispatch* recorded.[10]

Now a man without a party, Tyler felt free to endorse the admission of Texas to the Union. He was inadvertently aided by Great Britain. British emancipation of slaves in the West Indies had been a financial disaster, and London wanted to regain its economic position in the Caribbean and the Gulf of Mexico by adding Texas to the British Empire. However, the prospect of Texans pledging loyalty to the British crown did not stop Republican John Quincy Adams from opposing Texas's joining the Union.

Adams was by then a member of the U.S. House of Representatives. He converted to the anti-slavery cause only late in his career, but at age seventy-six, he saw the "Slave Power" conspiracy everywhere. He believed the South planned to annex Texas, divide it into four or five states, and give the South a permanent majority in the Senate. He and his cronies again threatened secession. As a result, they were able to prevent Tyler and his Secretary of State, John C. Calhoun, from obtaining the two-thirds majority in the Senate necessary for annexation.

Left: John Tyler, c. 1826, when he was governor of Virginia. *Courtesy of Virginia Historical Society;* Right: John Quincy Adams, c. 1845. *Courtesy of the National Archives*

In 1844, Whig frontrunner Henry Clay met privately with Democratic frontrunner Martin Van Buren. They agreed to drop Texas annexation as a campaign issue by offering separate statements against letting the Lone Star republic into the Union. This maneuver backfired on Van Buren because the South deserted him, and he was not able to get the two-thirds majority necessary to secure his party's nomination. Even Andrew Jackson, who was now old and dying, withdrew his support and backed James K. Polk, a former governor of Tennessee and a strong annexationist. To assuage the North, the Democrats brilliantly looked to balance the scale by admitting Oregon. With the Democrats supporting annexation, President Tyler now had no issue, so he withdrew from the race and endorsed Polk.

Polk won an extremely close election in November 1844. Interpreting this as a mandate, Tyler proposed a joint resolution to admit Texas into the Union because it only required a majority vote, not two-thirds. Backed by the Democrats, Tyler's resolution passed on a strict party-line vote, and President Tyler signed the admission on March 1, 1845—three days before he left office.

A major factor in the Whigs' defeat was the Tariff of 1842, which they managed to push through Congress and persuaded a reluctant President Tyler to sign. Called the Black Tariff, it raised the rates from 20 percent to nearly 40 percent. The tariff hamstrung the economy so severely that total tariff revenues declined. As a result, the Whigs lost both branches of Congress in 1844.

As soon as the United States annexed Texas, Mexico broke diplomatic relations with the U.S. The Mexican-American War followed (1846–48), in which the United States Army pushed to the Pacific and captured California and the modern Southwest.

Representative David Wilmot was an anti-slavery Democrat from northeastern Pennsylvania. He stirred the sectional cauldron again on August 8, 1846, by attaching a rider to an appropriations bill, saying that slavery would be prohibited in any territory annexed from Mexico.

He called slavery "... this 'peculiar institution' that belongs in the South."[11] The rider was called the "Wilmot Proviso."

Wilmot's measure made the Southerners angry because a disproportionate number of the volunteers who fought in Mexico came from Dixie. Southerners believed the proviso would cheat them out of equal access to a region they had conquered.

The House of Representatives was now more anti-Southern than ever. It passed the Wilmot Proviso several times in various forms, only to see it fail in the Senate.

Calhoun—who was always ready to lead the South—declared that Congress had no constitutional right to restrict slavery, despite the Missouri Compromise or the earlier Northwest Ordinance. He argued that the territories were owned by the United States and were "held jointly for their common use."[12] He asserted that only when a territory was ready for statehood could it constitutionally outlaw slavery.

The first photograph ever taken of a president and his cabinet, White House dining room, 1846. Left to right are John Y. Mason, attorney general; William L. Marcy, secretary of war; President Polk; and Robert Walker, the incredibly successful secretary of the treasury. Back row, left to right: Cave Johnson, postmaster general; and George Bancroft, secretary of the navy. Secretary of State James Buchanan is absent. *Courtesy of John Plumbe, White House Museum*

While Calhoun had a point, legally speaking, President Polk was also right, practically speaking. He considered the entire debate a dangerous abstraction because there was no way black slavery was going to take root in the dry climate of the Southwest. It just wasn't economically workable there, except maybe in the mining industry. Polk accused both Northern and Southern interests of trying to inflame and exploit the slavery issue for their own political gain. Senator James G. Blaine of Maine recalled: "The whole controversy over the Territories, as remarked by a witty representative from the South, related to an imaginary negro in an impossible place."[13]

The Southern leadership should never have made such a big issue out of an abstract concept. The abolitionist agitators were more than happy to squabble with them over it, and so the South lost political capital over an issue in which they had no hope of success in the first place. Simply, the arid and semi-arid West was never going to be fertile ground for plantation agriculture. The same sort of situation existed vis-à-vis the fugitive slave laws. There were few fugitive slaves (never more than 1,000 a year[14] out of 3,200,000 slaves in 1850 and only 803 fugitives out of 3,953,760 slaves in 1860),[15] but the controversy stirred up by the abolitionists, and later Republican newspapers reported as if there were a fugitive slave crisis every day. The unsophisticated, semi-literate immigrant who did not understand nineteenth-century fake news or know much American history was easy to mislead. There were millions of these in the 1840s and 1850s, and they took the abolitionists' hoopla seriously.

● ● ●

The Tariff of 1842 had been a disaster. Treasury Secretary Robert J. Walker was President Polk's point man assigned the task of repairing the damage. Walker drafted a report and suggested dropping the rates to pre-1842 levels, that is, from around 40 percent to about 25 percent. Congress enacted his recommendations in 1846. This measure coincided with Britain's repeal of its Corn Laws (restrictions on grain imports by the U.K.) and led to a trade boom worldwide. Even though rates were slashed, net revenue collected grew from $30,000,000 per year under the Black Tariff to nearly $45,000,000 per year under the "Walker Tariff," as the Tariff of 1846 was called. It materially contributed to the economic boom the United States experienced in the 1840s and 1850s and remained in effect until the passage of the Tariff of 1857, which used the 1846 tariff as a base.[16] Only the iron manufacturers of Pennsylvania and the wool producers of New England and the West opposed the 1857 Tariff. It remained in effect until the Deep South seceded.

Meanwhile, the Whigs nominated General Zachary Taylor of Louisiana for president in 1848, though his political views were generally unknown. All he had recommending him was his fame as a war hero. His running mate was Millard Filmore. The Democratic nominee, U.S. Senator Lewis Cass of Michigan, ran on a platform of "popular sovereignty," that it should be left up to the residents of a particular territory whether slavery should be permitted there or not.[17] The Free Soilers, a major third party, nominated Martin Van Buren. Charles Francis Adams, John Quincy Adams' son, was his vice-presidential pick.

The so-called "barn burners," who supported the Wilmot Proviso, split the Democratic vote in the North.

The election was close and heated. The Southern slaveholders were called the "Lords of the Lash," while their opponents (northern textile manufacturers) were dubbed the "Lords of the Loom." Many of the Free Soil Democrats wanted to keep the west open for free white laborers. Congressman Wilmot told one rally: "The negro race already occupy enough of this fair continent. Let us keep what remains for ourselves... for free white labor."[18]

Both major candidates carried fifteen states. Taylor received 47.3 percent of the popular vote while Cass got 42.5 percent. Van Buren took 10.1 percent of the popular vote but carried no states. Taylor won 163 votes in the Electoral College to Cass's 127.

Meanwhile, since the discovery of gold in 1848, California's population increased rapidly. In 1849, it was still under military rule but wanted statehood. President Taylor approved and encouraged it to bypass the territorial stage and apply for direct admission into the Union. The problem was that there were fifteen slave states and fifteen free states. If California were admitted, it would forever tilt the balance of power in the Senate against the South.

In November 1849, California passed an anti-slavery constitution. New Mexico followed suit. Seeing power shifting to the hostile North, a few Southern leaders talked seriously about secession for the first time.

This was the final act in the Senate for the "Great Triumvirate": Henry Clay, John C. Calhoun, and Daniel Webster. On January 29, 1850, Clay proposed his last, great compromise. It would occupy Congress' time for the next seven months.[19] It provided for California to be admitted to the Union as a free state. The rest of the Mexican conquest would be organized into the territories of New Mexico and Utah, which would decide the slavery issue themselves under the doctrine of popular sovereignty. Texas would cede its disputed lands to New Mexico in exchange for the United States paying off the state's debt of $10,000,000 ($276,000,000 in 2017 dollars). The slave trade would be outlawed in the District of Columbia, but slavery would not be, and the fugitive slave law would be strengthened and enforced.

On March 4, Calhoun presented his last speech, twenty-seven days before his death. He was so ill with tuberculous that he had to sit wrapped in a blanket while his colleague, James Mason of Virginia, read the speech. He warned that an overbearing North was dissolving the ties that held the states together. The United States, he declared, could not hold together by cries of "Union, Union, glorious Union," any more than a physician could save a seriously ill patient by crying "Health, health, glorious health." He exclaimed that compromise with Yankees was useless. The North would just use it as a stepping-stone to greater concessions later. Only the North, which was politically stronger, could save the Union by agreeing to a full and final settlement on the basis of just answers to all the questions now facing the two sections. But it was not doing this. The Northern press was mostly hostile to the South, its institutions, its morals, and its way of life. The Northern majority had already begun to construe the Constitution to increase federal power and diminish states' rights, to minimize Southern influence at the national level. To avert disunion, the North had to stop its attacks and agree to a constitutional amendment to protect the Southern minority. If it would not or could not, the South should leave in peace.[20]

Had it not been for Calhoun's full-throated embrace of slavery, he would have gone down in history as one of the greatest American political thinkers of all time, ranking just behind Jefferson. Even so, John F. Kennedy ranked him among the top five senators ever. Had the South listened to Calhoun, the Civil War would have been fought a decade earlier, when the South was stronger. During the next ten years, due to immigration and the development of the West, the North grew stronger while Southern strength lagged. The South had a much better chance of winning in 1850 than it did in 1861, and even then, it was a near-run thing. But Southern leaders did not wish to listen to Calhoun's sage advice in 1850, and this fact made a huge difference in the outcome of the war.

Webster made his final speech three days after Calhoun. He endorsed Clay's compromise.[21] The anti-slavery Whigs, led by Senator William H. Seward of New York, were disappointed. Seward, meanwhile, became metaphysical. He spoke of obeying a "higher law" than the Constitution—the kind of argument that could justify anything.

Zachary Taylor was a prosperous planter and a victorious general, but he was an unsophisticated politician. By the spring of 1850, he had fallen under Seward's influence and was prepared to veto the compromise, but he never got the chance because the Senate rejected it. It then appeared that the United States was heading for another sectional impasse, but on the Fourth of July, Taylor consumed a large amount of raw fruit and iced milk during the holiday celebrations at the Washington Monument, which was then under construction. Several cabinet members became ill of an unknown intestinal disorder, as did the president. He died on July 9, and Millard Fillmore succeeded him.

Left: Zachary Taylor. *Courtesy of Heritage Auction Galleries;* Right: Taylor's vice president, Millard Fillmore. *Courtesy of the Library of Congress*

Unlike his predecessor, Fillmore was a veteran politician, having served as comptroller of New York, congressman, chairman of the powerful Ways and Means Committee, and vice president. Unlike Taylor, he supported the compromise.

After a disappointed Henry Clay went home to recuperate from the exhausting debate (he would die from Tuberculosis in 1852), Senator Stephen A. Douglas of Illinois became the leader. He successfully guided the compromise through the Senate piece by piece instead of as a whole measure. The free state majority in the House of Representatives now backed off their earlier opposition in order to secure the admission of California without provoking the South to secession. By September 1850, all pieces were passed by Congress and signed by President Fillmore.

Despite Fillmore's hopes, the Compromise of 1850 was not a permanent solution. The so-called Southern fire-eaters reserved for themselves the right of secession, and their candidates were only narrowly defeated in four elections that winter. Eventually, the anti-slavery Whigs managed to block President Fillmore's nomination for reelection in 1852, in part because of a best-selling novel.

The Northern abolitionists were bitterly disappointed by the Compromise of 1850 and continued to agitate. Although they did not always confine themselves to the truth, they were, without a doubt, propaganda masters. In June 1851, a fictional work appeared that inflamed the North. Called *Uncle Tom's Cabin*, it was written by Harriet Beecher Stowe, the daughter, sister, and wife of narrow-minded abolitionist preachers. It first appeared in serial form but was soon published as a huge bestselling novel. It sold more than 300,000 copies within a year, and more than one million including British Empire sales.

Uncle Tom's Cabin was both sentimental and melodramatic, as befitted nineteenth-century tastes. It was also world-class propaganda. The central theme was the evil and immorality of slavery and, by inference, the evil and immorality of the South. It magnified every horrible aspect of slavery. One slave woman named Prue, for example, is forced to let her child starve to death. In her misery, she takes to drinking, so Master beats her to death. The hero, Uncle Tom, is a noble and courageous Christian who stands up for his beliefs and is admired by his enemies. Today, "Uncle Tom" is an epithet for an African-American who sold out to the whites, but that is not how he appears in the book and certainly not how Stowe meant to depict him. In the novel, his cruel master, Simon Legree, who is a Northerner by birth, tries to break him of his religious faith. When he fails, Legree beats Tom to death out of frustration.

Simon Legree assaulting Uncle Tom. *Courtesy of Terry Borton, the American Magic Lantern Theater*

The novel unsettled and infuriated the North. Many of the less educated, less discriminating Northerners—especially the recent immigrants—
did not realize that the book was a work of fiction. Given the Northern
public reaction to it, it passed for nonfiction to many. Beginning with Vermont, nine free state legislatures voted to offer legal defense for fugitive slaves
and/or to ignore federal law altogether. Although they did not use the word,
they in effect nullified the Fugitive Slave Law. William Lloyd Garrison
declared that Northern secession would be an excellent way to eliminate
this subsidy to slaveholders.[22] So significant was the impact of *Uncle Tom's
Cabin* on the North that, when he met her in 1861, Lincoln reportedly
greeted Stowe with the words: "So you're the little woman who wrote the
book that made this great war."[23]

Shortly after that, a Southerner played into the hands of the abolitionist
propagandists. Speaking about Bleeding Kansas on May 20, 1856, U.S. senator
Charles Sumner of Massachusetts launched an extremely vicious and hate-filled
personal attack on the character of Senator Andrew Butler of South Carolina.
The speech was full of sexual innuendo, which was standard, because the abolitionists routinely accused slaveholders of keeping the institution so that a regu-
lar supply of black women would be available for their sexual amusement.
Stephen Douglas, also verbally attacked by Sumner, muttered to a colleague,
"This damn fool is going to get himself shot by some other damn fool."

Douglas was not the only one to take exception to Sumner's remarks.
Representative Preston Brooks, who was related to Senator Butler, considered
challenging Sumner to a duel. He consulted with Representative Laurence M.
Keitt (also of South Carolina) about dueling etiquette. Keitt told him that not
everyone should fight a duel. Dueling was for gentlemen and men of equal
social standing. Sumner, Keitt declared, did not qualify as a gentleman. He
was no better than a drunkard, as his coarse language and vulgar insinuations
proved. It would be better to give the New Englander a caning.

On May 22, Brooks entered the Senate chamber, found Sumner sitting
at his desk, and beat him unconscious with his cane. Some of the senators
tried to help Sumner, but Keitt blocked them with a pistol. Sumner did not
return to the Senate until 1859, allegedly because his injuries were so severe.

The incident further polarized the country. Brooks was either a demon in the North or a hero in the South. To many Northerners, he was a real-life Simon Legree. The South, on the other hand, was quite pleased with Brooks' violence. For years, the abolitionists had been saying anything they wished, whether it was true or not, and very often it was not true. Sick and tired of the verbal abuse, many Southerners felt one of the leading abolitionists had gone too far and had gotten his comeuppance.

In the middle of the national uproar, Preston Brooks resigned his House seat and stood for reelection. He won a special election in August 1856 and reelection the following November for a full term. South Carolina voters had endorsed his actions. He died unexpectedly from a violent attack of croup on January 27, 1857. Despite horrible weather, thousands attended his memorial service and funeral.[24]

After the Brooks-Sumner incident, members of Congress in both chambers came to work armed.

The House of Representatives censured Laurence Keitt for his part in the Sumner caning. Keitt resigned at once and stood for reelection and won by an overwhelming margin. He remained in Congress until South Carolina seceded. In 1858, he unsuccessfully tried to choke a Pennsylvania congressman who insulted him. He served in the Provisional Confederate Congress (1861-62) before joining the army. He rose to the rank of colonel, commanded the Twentieth South Carolina Infantry Regiment and later Kershaw's Brigade after Brigadier General Joseph B. Kershaw became a divisional commander. Mortally wounded at Cold Harbor on June 1, 1864, Keitt died in Richmond on June 4.

Congressman Brooks repays an insult. *Courtesy of John Magee*

CHAPTER VIII

THE CHASM GROWS

*The great conflict will never be properly comprehended by
the man who looks upon it as a war for the preservation of
slavery.*

—*Robert Stiles, Yale graduate and Major of Artillery,
Army of Northern Virginia*

As the election of 1852 approached, no Democrat had enough support to garner the two-thirds of the delegates' votes necessary to secure the nomination. It looked as if Levi Woodbury of New Hampshire, associate justice of the Supreme Court,[1] would be the compromise nominee, but he died suddenly on September 4, 1851. When the convention met in Baltimore in June 1852, it deadlocked between Stephen A. Douglas, Senator Cass of Michigan, former secretary of war and former governor of New York William Marcy, James Buchanan of Pennsylvania, Sam Houston of Texas, Senator Benton of Missouri, and Franklin Pierce of New Hampshire. Pierce was selected as the compromise candidate on the forty-ninth ballot. He had not received a single vote on the first ballot or the thirty-fourth. When she heard the news, his wife was so upset she fainted.

Trying to duplicate their success of 1848, the Whigs nominated a war hero, General Winfield Scott, under whom Pierce served in Mexico. Because the Whigs could not unite their warring factions, they presented a party platform that was virtually indistinguishable from the Democrats. (Party platforms mattered more in those days.) This led to a complete lack of enthusiasm in the Northern anti-slavery faction and a low voter turnout. Pierce kept quiet and did not campaign personally. Scott should have followed Pierce's lead. He was not a good public speaker and committed gaffes often.

The Free Soil Party nominated Senator John P. Hale of New Hampshire, a staunch abolitionist whose daughter would later fall in love with and express a desire to marry John Wilkes Booth. The most famous Free Soiler, former President Martin Van Buren, had returned to the Democrats. The party took most of its votes from the Whigs. With 50.9 percent, Pierce won the popular vote, with 44.1 percent for Scott and 4.9 percent for Hale. Pierce carried twenty-seven states to Scott's four, and won two hundred fifty-four to forty-two in the Electoral College. The Democrats also won both houses of Congress.

According to most historians, Franklin Pierce was one of the worst and least successful presidents, though he had the potential to be so much more. He was personable, outgoing, and enjoyed socializing. But he also drank to excess, and it was said that he was the winner of many a hard-fought bottle. Early in his political life, he was a Jackson man. He started at the bottom as a town moderator; then he was state legislator, speaker of the state House of Representatives, congressman, and U.S. senator, becoming a young and rising star.

When the Mexican War began, he turned down an offer to be Polk's attorney general and volunteered for active field service. Already a colonel in the New Hampshire militia, he first led the Ninth U.S. Infantry Regiment and then his own brigade. Promoted to brigadier general in 1847, he was severely injured when his horse fell on him at Contreras and courageously fought the battle of Churubusco tied to his saddle. He took part in the battles of Molino del Rey and Chapultepec, as well as in the capture of Mexico City, and he returned home a war hero. He was practicing law in New Hampshire when he won the Democratic presidential nomination.

His wife was the opposite of Pierce: shy, withdrawn, reserved, devoutly religious (her father was a Congregational minister), and, contrary to her husband's drinking, pro-temperance. She suffered from ill health most of their marriage. Her maladies included severe depression, tuberculosis, and psychological issues. She also hated Washington, D.C., which caused stress in their marriage.

History often turns on a dime. One such turn occurred on January 6, 1853. The President-elect and his wife were traveling from Boston when their train derailed. It rolled down an embankment near Andover, Massachusetts. Pierce and his wife survived, but their only living child, Benjamin or "Benny," was crushed to death and nearly decapitated.[2] Pierce could not prevent his wife from seeing the body. Afterward, both Pierces suffered from depression, Jane greatly. She wondered if Benny's death was God's punishment for her husband's seeking high office. A cloud came over their marriage and Pierce's incoming administration. His son's death and Jane's constant depression continued to trouble Franklin and materially contributed to the failure of his administration. Pierce was already a heavy drinker; after, he drank even more. It would eventually kill him. Franklin Pierce died of cirrhosis of the liver in 1869. His wife died of depression six years before him.

Franklin and Jane Pierce. *Courtesy of the Library of Congress*

Despite the gloom in the White House, the 1850s were years of great national prosperity. Track mileage increased from 9,021 to 30,627 miles, and railroads became America's first billion-dollar industry.[3] There was a considerable amount of talk at this time about building a transcontinental railroad from California with connections all the way to the east coast.

Pierce's secretary of war, Jefferson Davis, took the lead by ordering two routes surveyed, one north and one south. U.S. ambassador to Mexico James Gadsden negotiated a $10,000,000 purchase of land to help the southern route. It was undoubtedly the more logical of the two. The territory through which it would pass was already organized, the Indian claims had been settled, and the terrain was easier for railroad construction. The northern route would have to cross difficult parts of the Rocky Mountains, the Indian claims would have to be settled or the tribes slaughtered and forcefully removed, much of the area was not open to white settlement, and the territory was not organized. There was a great deal of money involved, however, so Senator Douglas and his special interest groups and moneyed cronies wanted a northern route to go through Chicago. With this in his mind, Douglas introduced a bill to organize Kansas and Nebraska as territories. The Missouri Compromise had outlawed slavery in those territories many years before, but Douglas needed Southern support to pass his bill. For this reason, he included in his bill the principle of popular sovereignty, favored by the South, where territories alone decided to admit slavery or not. This revoked the Missouri Compromise which outlawed slavery north of the southern Missouri border (excluding Missouri, of course). Finally, Douglas proposed the transcontinental railroad would be built and owned by private (Northern) interests, financed by public land grants.

Historian Allan Nevins called Stephen A. Douglas "a ferocious fighter, the fiercest, most ruthless, and most unscrupulous that Congress had perhaps ever known."[4] He pressured President Pierce into supporting the proposal, even though he was not enthusiastic about repealing the Missouri Compromise, but he did so at Douglas's insistence. Jefferson Davis and Secretary of the Navy James C. Dobbin of North Carolina also supported repeal because they erroneously thought Kansas would be admitted to the Union as a slave state, thus keeping the balance of power in the Senate.

The Kansas-Nebraska Act was fraught with unintended consequences. Horace Greeley, an abolitionist leader and the editor of the *New York Tribune*, later commented that the act created more abolitionists in two months than William Lloyd Garrison produced in twenty years. The fatal flaw was that the act required the Yankees to become actively involved in capturing and returning fugitive slaves, and it ripped the scab off the national slavery wound. Rallies were held against the peculiar institution throughout the North. Feeling that their leaders had been bamboozled, many Northerners, who had until now been anti-slavery but not strongly so, suddenly forgot their ancestors' involvement in human bondage and became fervently abolitionist.

Stephen A. Douglas, the "Little Giant." *Courtesy of the Library of Congress*

The Southern leadership in Congress made a terrible mistake in supporting this bill. Their aim in doing so was to keep the balance of power in the Senate, but that was not going to happen. The climate of Kansas and Nebraska was not conducive to plantation agriculture, and slavery would never have worked there. The Missouri Compromise had kept the issue largely dormant for over thirty years, and Southern leaders had no real chance at making Kansas a Southern state. All they succeeded in accomplishing was inflaming passions throughout the nation, alienating North from South, starting a low-intensity civil war in Missouri and Kansas, and polarizing the country for no practical purpose.

One must also consider that what it meant to be a Northerner was changing. They were still just as "anti-Negro" as ever, but many of them were recent arrivals from the Old World: they were mostly Irish and German, but there were smaller groups from other parts of the world too. They had little education and were easily misled by abolitionist propaganda. There were no black slaves where they came from, and they had little tolerance for slavery in their new home—unlike the New Englanders of the past.

The campaign of 1854 ended in a landmark election. Both the Democrats and Whigs lost a substantial number of seats in Congress. Of their one hundred fifty-eight seats in the House (out of two hundred thirty-four), the Democrats lost eighty-three seats (over half!) and their majority. Only seven of the fifty-four Northern Democrats who voted for Douglas' Kansas-Nebraska Act kept their positions. The American or "Know Nothing" Party, which was formed out of anti-Catholic and anti-immigrant elements, went from zero to fifty-one seats. They soon allied with the anti-slavery Opposition Party and a few smaller parties, which held a handful of seats.

As a result of this election, the Whig Party collapsed. For a time, it was not clear if the former Whigs would join the Know-Nothings or the newly formed anti-slave Republican Party as the leading political party in the North. The Know-Nothings, however, made the same mistake as the Whigs. They looked to attract both Northern and Southern support by evading the slavery issue. This approach did not work. Most of the former Northern Whigs joined the Republicans, which became the first genuinely regional party in the United States. It was a big government, big business party from the beginning. It advanced the ideas of Hamilton, who believed these policies would bring national growth through a powerful centralized government and government intervention through government regulation, subsidies, and high tariff policies, rather than through free-market solutions.

Meanwhile, the House of Representatives could not elect a speaker. Eventually, its members agreed to pick a plurality speaker. In a major coup, Nathaniel P. Banks, a Republican from Massachusetts, secured election on the 133rd ballot. It was the first time a Republican held national office.

Although he later proved to be a poor Union general, even Southerners, such as future Confederate vice president Alexander Stephens and former speaker Howell Cobb, were fond of the smooth and charming Banks, and he turned out to be a more effective speaker than many anticipated. He funneled money into the coffers of the railroads and later, after three terms as governor of Massachusetts, was offered a lucrative job: president of the Illinois Central Railroad.

● ● ●

As the election approached and it became evident that the political winds were shifting, the political chameleons naturally changed with them. Abraham Lincoln, for example, became less moderate. As an attorney, he had represented a slave owner and argued to have his client's slaves, who had fled to Illinois, returned to him. (He lost the case.) He had been silent on the issue of slavery, he had supported the Black Codes, and he was a big believer in African colonialization. In 1854, he was an extraordinarily successful and wealthy corporate attorney, but his political career was at a low point. Now, instead of proposing a moral and even-handed solution to the problem, he demonized the South and said they were likely to expand slavery to the West. This claim was absurd, and Lincoln had to know it (there were only eighty-five slaves in Kansas at its peak), but being the political opportunist that he was, he joined the chorus anyway. This sort of thing happened across the North as the abolitionists whipped crowds into mass hysteria. To Northerners, keeping slavery out of the territories seemed like an excellent way to keep blacks out of the West altogether.[5]

In this overheated emotional climate, the "Border War" began. The New England Aid Company was created to colonize Kansas with Free-Stater Northern immigrants. Simultaneously, the "Border Ruffians" from Missouri crossed the state line. Their leader was U.S. senator David R. Atchison, a big slaveholder, who wanted another Southern state in the Senate and Kansas to have a rigid slave code so it would never be a refuge for fugitive slaves (like his own runaways). Many Southerners felt that their future depended upon gaining another Southern (slave) state in the Senate. They were wrong. Minnesota and Oregon were already preparing to enter the Union as non-slave states. The South had already lost the demographic race. Characteristically, however, it was slow to admit defeat and to seek other political options.

During the state election of 1855, Missouri natives crossed the border and (according to Northern newspapers) stuffed the ballot boxes with thousands of fraudulent votes. They elected a legislature that made opposing slavery a felony and aiding a fugitive slave a capital offense. The Pierce administration backed the pro-slavery faction.

In 1855, abolitionists, Northern immigrants, and assorted Free-Staters met in Topeka and drew up the so-called Topeka Constitution, which outlawed slavery in Kansas. Skirmishing between the factions continued, with people verbally abused, assaulted, beaten, shot, and killed. In May 1856, 700 pro-Southern men descended on Lawrence, Kansas, and pillaged the place. Shortly thereafter, fanatical abolitionist John Brown retaliated by torturing and murdering five Southerners. They were not slave holders and had not taken part in the Lawrence Raid. That whole summer was marked by multiple barn burnings, house burnings, ambushes, and bushwhacking. At least 200 people were killed. Property damage ran into the millions.[6] This would all continue, with varying degrees of intensity, until 1865.

In 1857, the pro-slavery factions met in the provisional capital of Lecompton and drafted the Lecompton Constitution, which allowed slavery. The new U.S. president, James Buchanan of Pennsylvania, strongly endorsed the Lecompton Constitution before Congress. Kansas held a referendum with both constitutions on the ballot. Many abolitionists boycotted the vote, and voter fraud took place on both sides. At least 6,000 fraudulent ballots were cast. Both constitutions were sent to Washington for approval by Congress. Senator Douglas and many of the Northern Democrats broke with the president and opposed the Lecompton Constitution. While Lecompton stalled in Congress, Kansas held another referendum on it. This time, the abolitionists did not boycott the election and overwhelmingly defeated Lecompton in January 1858. The following month, a convention of Free-Staters drafted the Leavenworth Constitution, outlawing slavery. It was replaced by the Wyandotte Constitution, which eventually made Kansas a free state. This did not occur until after the Deep South seceded in 1861.[7]

• • •

In the U.S. election of 1856, the Democrats passed over Franklin Pierce because they were afraid his association with Bleeding Kansas might cost them the election. They also ignored Douglas, who had damaged himself with the South, and nominated James Buchanan, a largely unknown party elder. He had been ambassador to the United Kingdom under Pierce and was not tainted, as others were, with the turmoil of the past few years. Their platform endorsed popular sovereignty without defining it, a neat political trick. It backed a limited, frugal, and non-interfering federal government. Their vice presidential nominee was John Cabell Breckinridge of Kentucky, a Southerner who was associated with Douglas.

The Republicans nominated another war hero: legendary explorer General John C. Fremont. He was a well-connected political neophyte who was married to the daughter of Missouri senator Thomas Hart Benton, but he had also never held political office.

The Republican platform called for high tariffs and for slavery to be excluded from the territories. This would keep them from the "troublesome presence of free Negroes," as Lincoln said.[8] Not one word was said about moral considerations. The motives were purely to protect the economic and political interests of the North and West at the expense of the South. Its strategy was to spread alarm in the North by proclaiming that "Slave Power" or the "Slaveocracy" intended to gain control of the government. First, it would (somehow) conquer the territories; then it would spread slavery to the North. It would make every state a slave state. This was absurd, of course, but hysteria can work.

The Know-Nothings and the remnants of the Whig Party nominated Millard Fillmore. They denounced the repeal of the Missouri Compromise and warned against the dangers of Catholicism and sectionalism. They lessened their hostility to immigrants. Other than that, they had no real platform other than vague sentiments about a rapprochement on the issue of slavery.

The inauguration of James Buchanan, March 4, 1857. This is the first photograph of a presidential inauguration. *Courtesy of the Library of Congress*

In a sense, there were two elections: Buchanan vs. Fillmore in the South and Buchanan vs. Fremont in the North. The Republican party launched a vehement anti-slavery campaign. The Democrats pointed to the strong possibility that the Union would dissolve if the Republicans won, and this enabled them to carry five Northern states (Illinois, Indiana, Pennsylvania, New Jersey, and Delaware). Coupled with all the Southern states except Maryland, Buchanan garnered 174 electoral votes against Fremont's 114. Millard Fillmore took only Maryland and its eight electoral votes.

Even though they were the only national party, the Democrats received just 45 percent of the popular vote. Fremont carried all but five of the free states.

After the election, a coalition of Southern Democrats and Northern conservatives passed the Tariff of 1857. It reduced the duties to almost free-trade levels. The Republicans, supported by special interest groups such as the railroads and the New England manufacturers, proposed much more burdensome tariffs and were defeated—for now. They did, however, make the South fearful. Their proposed tariff would more than double the duties, if it were ever passed, and would result in economic devastation for Dixie.

● ● ●

Meanwhile, the United States Supreme Court issued one of its most famous landmark decisions. Dred Scott was a slave. His owner, an army doctor named John Emerson, took Scott with him when he was stationed in the free state of Illinois for two years and then to the free territory of Wisconsin for four years. When he returned to Missouri, Scott sued for his freedom.

Chief Justice Roger Taney was a Maryland Democrat and had been Jackson's secretary of the treasury. He had freed his slaves thirty years earlier, but on March 6, 1857, Taney and his colleagues ruled in favor of the slave owner. Speaking for the majority, Judge Taney declared that, because he was black, Scott was not a person under the U.S. Constitution; he was the property of his owner, and property could not be taken from anyone without due process of law. He also ruled that the Missouri Compromise's prohibition on slavery was unconstitutional. Congress had no right to exclude slavery from any of the territories, he ruled, and thus made the extreme Southern position the law of the land. Taney added that black people were "altogether unfit" to associate with white people, that they were "far inferior" to whites, and "they had no rights which the white man was bound to respect."[9]

Left: Chief Justice Roger Taney (1777–1864). *Courtesy of the Library of Congress;* Right: President James Buchanan (1791–1868). *Courtesy of the Library of Congress*

Not for the last time, many people hoped that the Supreme Court would find a solution to a regional problem that had evaded Congress, but the court only inflamed tensions. The Dred Scott Decision also undercut the doctrine of popular sovereignty (territories and states now had to admit slavery) and weakened the Douglas wing of the Democratic party. This was a tough break for Senator Douglas, who was now fighting for his political survival against the slick corporate lawyer Abraham Lincoln.

● ● ●

In 1858, Illinois was a state not unfriendly to the South. Much of its population had emigrated from slave states, including Lincoln himself, who was born in Kentucky. He even went so far as publicly declaring some sympathy for Dixie on slavery, remarking that the South would not embrace slavery today (i.e., 1858) if it were not already economically entrenched there. (He was correct on this point.) But the Dred Scott decision, the Lecompton Constitution, and "Bleeding Kansas" caused many Illinoisans to alter their pro-Southern positions. Nor were they particularly happy with the repeal of the Missouri Compromise or the Kansas-Nebraska Act.

The most historic part of the 1858 campaign for the Illinois Senate seat was the Lincoln-Douglas debates. The two opponents met seven times. Douglas attacked Lincoln's racist credentials. He accused Lincoln of thinking the black was his equal and hence his brother. Douglas himself pointedly remarked that the African American was not his equal and certainly not his brother.

Lincoln responded that he was not and never had been in favor of the equality of the races. He believed that so long as the two races lived together, there must be one superior race and one inferior race. "I, as much as any other man, am in favor of having the superior position assigned to the white race," he declared.[10]

Having successfully defended his racist credentials, Lincoln went on the attack. The climax occurred at Freeport on August 27, 1858. The Dred Scott Decision had placed Douglas in an untenable position, and his challenger recognized this and took full advantage of the fact. Douglas was a great believer in following the rulings of the courts. Lincoln shrewdly asked Douglas when exactly could a territory, prior to statehood, not admit slavery? Taney's decision said that they could never do so as a territory. Douglas's doctrine of popular sovereignty held that the people of a territory had the right to exclude or admit slavery as they pleased. Douglas was on the horns of a dilemma. He could renounce the Dred Scott Decision and offend the South or renounce popular sovereignty and jeopardize his reelection bid in Illinois. He chose the first way.

Douglas' dilemma cost him the popular vote that year; but, luckily for him, that was not a factor in 1858. Prior to the ratification of the

Seventeenth Amendment in 1913, state legislatures selected U.S. Senators. Voters did not cast ballots directly for Lincoln or Douglas but for state senators and/or representatives supporting either candidate. Only half the legislators were up for election in 1858. A slight majority of the voters cast their ballots for the tall Republican, but the Illinois General Assembly met on January 5, 1859, and reelected Stephen A. Douglas along a party-line vote of fifty-four to forty-six.

As a result of the election, Lincoln rose to national prominence. Also, slavery became a major issue. Prior to this campaign, Northern candidates avoided talking about slavery. Lincoln and Douglas spoke of little else.

The Buchanan Cabinet, circa 1859. Left to right: Jacob Thompson, secretary of the interior and future Confederate colonel; Lewis Cass, secretary of state; John B. Floyd, secretary of war and future Confederate general; Buchanan; Howell Cobb, secretary of the treasury and future Confederate general; Isaac Toucey, secretary of the navy; Joseph Holt, postmaster general and future Union general; and Jeremiah S. Black, attorney general and later secretary of state. Holt also served as secretary of war (1860–61). *Courtesy of Matthew Brady*

CHAPTER IX

JOHN BROWN, TERRORIST AND LIGHTNING ROD

I am heart and soul for the South. She is right in principle, and from the Constitution.

—*John Reynolds, governor of Illinois from 1830–1834*

It was Monday, October 17, 1859, in Arlington, Virginia, and Colonel Robert E. Lee was working on the financial accounts of his late father-in-law, George Washington Custis. When he died, Custis left Lee as the executor of his estate, which was both unprofitable and an entangled mess. The colonel would have been pleasantly surprised to see Lieutenant James E. B. "Jeb" Stuart. Young Stuart had been one of Lee's favorite cadets when Lee was superintendent of the U.S. Military Academy at West Point in the early 1850s.

The handsome Stuart looked different. He was clean shaven at "the Point" but now sported a huge beard likely to hide his lantern jaw. Stuart's father had been a lawyer who was famous locally as a *bon vivant* and heavy drinker. Jeb, who was also known as "Beauty," grew up under his mother's influence. He was a teetotaler and a devout Episcopalian, although (like Lee) he did enjoy flirting with the ladies.

Stuart married the daughter of Colonel Philip St. George Cooke (a future Union general),[2] and Jeb and his wife were each given a slave as a personal servant. The Stuarts did not believe in slavery and quickly freed both of the African Americans. Posted to the Kansas frontier, Jeb fought the Cheyenne. One of them shot him in the chest just as the lieutenant struck the Indian in the head with his sword, but the bullet missed any vital organs, and Stuart recovered rapidly.[3] He and his men also were part of a peacekeeping force attempting to mitigate the violence between John Brown and other abolitionist hooligans and the Missouri "Border Ruffians." (As history shows, they were not successful.) Like Lee, Stuart was on leave in 1859, and there were several things he wanted to do during the break. First, he and his wife wanted to show their first child to her relatives. Then he wanted to attend the Episcopal Church's General Convention as a lay delegate. There were business opportunities too. On that Monday morning, he had intended to stop by the War Department in Washington, D.C., looking to sell a device he invented. Designed for attaching a saber to a horseman's belt, he called it "Stuart's Lightning Horse Hitcher." Instead of his scheduled appointment, however, his orders were to go to Arlington to fetch Colonel Lee. There was a serious disturbance in the Harper's Ferry area. On hearing the news from Stuart, Lee left at once. He did not even bother to put on his uniform.

When he arrived in D.C., Secretary of War John Floyd and President Buchanan told Lee that a man calling himself Smith and some "Kansas 'Free-Staters'" were inciting a slave insurrection at Harper's Ferry and seized the government arsenal. The governors of Maryland and Virginia had already ordered state militiamen to the Ferry. The commander of Fort Monroe, Virginia, was sending a battalion, while a detachment of U.S. Marines in Washington was preparing to move, and ninety sailors from the Norfolk Naval Yard were on railroad cars, heading northwest. Lee's orders were to take command of all these forces and put down the revolt. Lieutenant Stuart offered to serve as a volunteer aide, and Colonel Lee accepted. The two future Rebel generals left D.C. by a special train at five o'clock p.m.

It was later learned that "Smith" was an alias used by John Brown, with whom Stuart had skirmished in Kansas. Born in Connecticut in 1800, John Brown was the descendant of Puritans. He was a failure in life, and as Dr. Ludwell H. Johnson wrote, "in ordinary times he would have been interesting mainly in a clinical sense."[4] He became a fanatical abolitionist and recruited a small following. After securing funding in New England and Ohio, Brown went west, where he and his people took part in the turmoil that was "Bleeding Kansas," and murdered five men in cold blood, most hacked to death by swords in front of their screaming wives and children. After briefly making their living by robbery and cattle rustling, Brown and his gang fled Kansas for New England, where he obtained funding for a terrorist attack in Virginia. He intended to seize the U.S. arsenal at Harper's Ferry, secure weapons, gather followers, and foment a slave rebellion throughout the South. He intended to push southwest through the Great Valley formed by the Appalachian Mountains, gaining both black and white recruits as he went, spreading terror, rallying the slaves, gathering supplies, and killing and burning all the way. Brown believed there were 100,000 muskets in the arsenal. A Connecticut company provided him with 950 pikes. He also had one hundred ninety-eight .52 caliber breech-loading Sharps carbines and an assortment of other weapons.

Brown believed he would receive 200 to 500 black recruits the first day, with more arriving every hour. Word of the rebellion, he convinced himself, would spread like wildfire. By the time the state militias of Virginia and Maryland reacted, Brown speculated, his forces would outnumber them. He had a poor opinion of the militia in any case.

Among others, he tried to recruit Frederick Douglass and an ex-slave named Shields Green, whom he met in a quarry near Chambersburg, Pennsylvania. "Emperor" Green joined the raiders, but Douglass made a more intelligent decision. He looked upon the raid as a suicide mission. He warned Brown against the attack, saying "You will never get out alive!"[5]

Abolitionist Harriett Tubman also consented to help Brown and recruited slaves in southern Ontario to join the invasion. (Brown liked her and called her "General" Tubman.) As the day for the attack approached, however, she disappeared. Historians disagree as to whether she was ill or in hiding because she, like Douglass, had doubts as to the raid's chances of success.

Frederick Douglass was right. Harper's Ferry lay in a bowl between three mountains and was impossible to defend. Nor were the African-Americans here badly treated compared to those on some of the cotton, tobacco, and rice plantations of the Deep South. There were no true plantations in this mountainous region. Most of the area's blacks were house servants and free people of color. They would not be enthusiastic about joining a dubious revolt. Brown was counting on their support, but he would not get it, and everything depended on speed. Brown had to form the core of his army before Virginia, Maryland, and the federal government could react.

Left: Jeb Stuart. *Courtesy of the National Archives;* Right: John Brown. *Courtesy of the Library of Congress*

Brown assumed the alias "Isaac Smith" and rented the Kennedy farmhouse about four miles north of Harper's Ferry. Here, he assembled twenty-two men and his weapons cache and made his final preparations. On the night of Sunday, October 16, he struck.

At first, all went well. They captured Colonel Lewis Washington, the great-grandnephew of President Washington, at his Beall-Air Estate. Brown (who admired George Washington) stole the sword sent to the general by Frederick the Great, as well as a brace of pistols given to the president by Marquis de Lafayette. The terrorists took several hostages and "liberated" several slaves, although none of these had any interest in joining such a half-baked operation. Meanwhile, the raiders seized the arsenal.

The first casualty occurred when Hayward Shepherd, a highly respected free man of color and a baggage master for the Baltimore and Ohio Railroad, realized what was happening. Rather than join the raiders, he tried to run away, so Brown's men shot him in the back. Shepherd died of his wounds. Also murdered was Thomas Boerly, an arsenal worker on his way to work.[6]

In the meantime, Brown's people captured a B&O train, which was passing through Harper's Ferry. For unknown reasons, Brown let the train go ahead. This was a foolish mistake. The train's crew and passengers spread the word downline that abolitionists had seized Harper's Ferry. Individual militia companies from nearby communities quickly assembled and joined the fray. Local black people refused to join the battle, but local whites did—against Brown. Three more civilians were killed in the sporadic firing, including the unarmed mayor, Fontaine Beckham,[7] and George W. Turner, who had attended West Point with Robert E. Lee.[8] Brown and his men took refuge in the armory, which was soon surrounded by local farmers and shopkeepers. Before long, they realized how few men Brown had, and they recaptured the arsenal and loosely surrounded the terrorists in the nearby fire engine house.

Lee and Stuart arrived on the Maryland side of Harper's Ferry about ten o'clock p.m. Lee, Stuart, and about ninety marines under the command of Lieutenant Israel Greene walked across the dark railroad bridge to the armory where Colonel Lee decided to wait until daylight to attack. He sent Jeb Stuart to demand "Smith" surrender. Stuart entered the engine room, startled at what he saw. "Why, aren't you old Osawatomie Brown of Kansas, whom I once had there as my prisoner?"

"Yes, but you did not keep me," he responded.

Recovering from his surprise, Stuart told him to surrender, but Brown responded that he knew what that meant—a rope for himself and his men. "I prefer to die just here," he said.[9] Stuart answered that he would return early in the morning for a final reply. After he left, Brown and his men barricaded the doors and blocked the windows.

At first light on October 18, Stuart again advanced to the engine house double doors under a flag of truce. "Are you ready to surrender, and trust to the mercy of the government?" he asked.

"No," Brown responded. "I prefer to die here." But he also tried to negotiate. He wanted to pass through Lee's lines into Maryland with his men and wagons, where he promised to release his hostages, but the lieutenant refused to bargain.

Several of the hostages and captured workmen cried out to Lee and Stuart, urging them not to use force or Brown would kill them. Above their voices came the roar of Colonel Washington: "Never mind us! *Fire!*"

"The old Revolutionary blood does tell," an admiring Robert E. Lee remarked. He was sitting on a horse, about fifteen yards from the firehouse.[10]

Stuart stepped aside and dropped his hat—the signal for the attack. A dozen Marines rushed forward with heavy hammers, but that did not work. The double doors held firm. Lieutenant Greene ordered his men to ram the doors with a heavy ladder nearby. The wooden doors splintered on the second ram. Greene rushed in, followed by his men. The two marines behind him were shot—one by Brown himself. Private Matthew Ruppert, who was shot in the face, survived, but Private Luke Quinn, shot by Brown in the abdomen, died. Colonel Washington, meanwhile, pointed Brown out to Greene. Ignoring the shower of bullets flying all around him, the marine lieutenant rushed the anti-slavery leader (who was kneeling to reload) and swung his saber hard, intent on splitting Brown's skull. "Osawatomie" dodged to the side at the last instant. The blow only left a deep gash in his neck. As Brown stood up, the lieutenant gave him an under-thrust with his sword midway up his body, lifting him completely off the ground. Fortunately for Brown, the thrust hit his belt buckle. Greene's sword then bent double, so he delivered several vicious blows to Brown's head with the hilt, using it as one might use brass knuckles.[11]

History, as we know, sometimes turns on a dime. The marines in Washington, D.C., had been stationed there primarily for ceremonial purposes. When turned out the day before, no one told them what their mission was. Assuming it was some sort of parade or ceremony involving dignitaries, Lieutenant Greene ordered his men to wear their dress uniforms, which meant he also wore his lighter, less lethal, dress sword to Harper's Ferry. If he been carrying his combat sword, Brown's splattered insides would have been all over the fire engine house's floor. There would never have been a John Brown trial, the South might not have realized how successful abolitionist propaganda had been in swaying Northern opinion, and they would not have known the depths of hatred many Northerners now had for them. Their reaction to the election of a Republican president in 1860 might have been different.[12]

The Marines storm the Harper's Ferry Engine House, 1859. *Courtesy of* Harpers Weekly, *November 1859*

As it was, Brown was severely wounded. He collapsed, and his rebellion collapsed with him. The Marines poured into the firehouse. One of them pinned an abolitionist to the wall with his bayonet.[13] Another terrorist crawled under a fire engine. A marine sent a bullet after him, ending his life. The remaining outlaws surrendered within a minute or two. The marines hauled Brown and his surviving men outside to the grass and treated their wounds. In all, ten abolitionists were dead—including two of Brown's sons—three were immediately captured, four were captured later, and five escaped. Six civilians died and nine were wounded, as were two marines, one fatally. There were militia casualties as well, but their exact numbers are not known.

Governor Henry A. Wise arrived later that day and personally interrogated Brown. Robert E. Lee was present. Afterwards, he commented that the entire effort was the "attempt of a fanatic or a madman." In his report, Lee called Brown and his men "rioters."[14]

Following the raid, investigators examined the Kennedy Farm. They found Brown's correspondence with the Secret Six, a.k.a. the Secret Committee of Six—the abolitionists who funded John Brown. They also discovered maps of Alabama, Florida, Georgia, Kentucky, Louisiana, Mississippi, South Carolina, North Carolina, and Tennessee. The maps had notes pasted to the margins showing the black population. Counties with predominantly African-American populations had been highlighted. They also found the provisional Constitution for Brown's new government and 900 pikes.

An ingenious pro-Secessionist agitator Edmund Ruffin got hold of some of the pikes and sent one to the legislature of each Southern state with the inscription: "Sample of the favors designed for us by our Northern Brethren."[15]

John Brown's trial rocked the nation. It began on October 27, 1859. The State of Virginia charged him with treason. He was defended by a team of New England lawyers, led by Massachusetts abolitionist John Albion Andrew. Brown masterfully turned the entire proceeding into a propaganda show, and in the mind of the North, he effectively put the South and slavery on trial. Twenty-two years later, Frederick Douglass said, "John Brown began the war that ended American slavery, and made this a free republic."[16]

Prosecuting Attorney Andrew Hunter wanted a speedy trial, and John Brown concurred. Everyone knew, including him, that he was guilty of murder and was going to hang. Even after conviction, Brown admitted that he had received a fair trial. His lawyers, realizing that any traditional legal defense was hopeless, ignored their client and pled insanity. Privately, his lawyers suggested methods of escape. Brown did not even consider escaping. He wanted to die a martyr. Martyrs who escape from jails lose credibility, he said.

The trial was held in the county seat of Charles Town. The verdict was handed down on October 30. Brown was guilty of treason, conspiring with and telling slaves to escape and revolt, and first-degree murder. Sentenced to death two days later, he was hanged on December 2, 1859. Shields "Emperor" Green was hanged on December 16. His body was given to the Winchester Medical College as a teaching cadaver.

The North's reaction to Brown's trial and execution shocked the South—especially the moderates. Church bells rang in his honor, women wore black mourning clothes, men wore black armbands, politicians lauded him, businesses closed, and ladies cried on the day of his execution. Henry David Thoreau and Wendell Phillips praised him, as did Ralph Waldo Emerson and the rest of the New England literary elite. Emerson declared that the inmates of the Massachusetts prison were superior human beings to the leaders of the South. Thoreau compared the fanatical old terrorist to Jesus Christ.[17] Others referred to him as "Saint John the Just."[18] Some Northerners came completely unhinged in their praise, hailing Brown as an angel of light and a St. John the Baptist. Critics castigated Senator Seward of New York for calling his execution "necessary and just."[19] Abraham Lincoln, who did not want the South to secede or to engage in civil war, called Brown "insane." (Later he flip-flopped on this sentiment as well. Senator Douglas introduced a measure to protect the constitutional rights of the states and punish those guilty of interstate insurrection, including the Brown terrorists. Lincoln delivered a speech in Cooper Union, New York, and denounced the Douglas Resolution as a "Sedition Bill.")[20]

Shortly after Brown's execution, his chief lawyer, John Albion Andrew, was elected governor of Massachusetts. This proved to the South that the

Republican party was not distancing itself from its extremist members but was embracing them. They looked on his election as endorsing anti-Southern violence and servile insurrection.

The Secret Six who funded Brown were Thomas Wentworth Higginson, Dr. Samuel G. Howe, Theodore Parker, Franklin B. Sanborn, Gerrit Smith, and George Luther Steams. Brown's captured documents and subsequent investigations of him revealed that they had financed the Harper's Ferry Raid, perhaps to the tune of $25,000 ($679,000 in 2017 dollars). Realizing that the jig was up, Howe, Sanborn, and Stearns fled to Canada to avoid arrest; Parker (who suffered from tuberculosis) had already gone to Italy for his health.[21] Gerrit Smith checked himself into a lunatic asylum and denied all connections with the Harper's Ferry Raid. Frederick Douglass, who knew of the planned attack, also fled to Canada. Only Higginson remained at large in the United States. A rabid abolitionist and Unitarian minister who advocated war to eradicate slavery, Higginson was involved in aiding abolitionist forces in Kansas and no doubt met John Brown there. He raised money for Brown's legal defense but was never tried.[22] He remained in Massachusetts, where he knew that he would not face arrest or extradition.

Seven of Brown's raiders were still at large. The Republican governors of Iowa and Ohio refused to extradite the felons, who had sought refuge there. Two of the outlaws fled to Pennsylvania and were apprehended. Pennsylvania governor William F. Parker, a Democrat, followed the law and only temporarily delayed the extradition because of an error in the paperwork. He ordered the raiders to be held in jail until the Old Dominion authorities could correct their mistake. Eventually extradited, the pair was tried and executed. Governor John Ellis of North Carolina held up this incident as "a practical illustration of the difference between a northern Democrat and a black Republican."[23]

The Northern governors' refusal to extradite the Harper's Ferry criminals and the outrage it produced in Dixie has received less attention than it deserves. To Southerners, it was proof that the North did not intend to insist on obedience to the law. To many, it was a harbinger of what to expect under Republican rule. Three Southern states (South Carolina, Georgia, and Texas) mentioned the refusal to extradite as one of their reasons for seceding.[24] When abolitionist thugs seized a Southern town, a Democrat president sent in the Marines. Could the South depend on a Republican president to react the same way under similar circumstances, Southern editors and the public wanted to know? They concluded that they could not. Many Union men, such as Professor Thomas Jonathan Jackson of the Virginia Military Institute, began to think seriously about embracing secession. Many Southern moderates started to believe the "fire-eaters" had been right all along. The country was now hopelessly at odds. It would only take the election of a Republican president to cause an explosion.

CHAPTER X

THE ELECTION
OF 1860

*The war between the North and the South is a tariff war. The
war is further, not for any principle, does not touch on the
question of slavery, and in fact turns on the Northern lust for
power.*

—*Karl Marx and Friedrich Engels*[1]

Radical Republicans professed not to follow the exact words of
the Constitution. New York Senator and radical Republican
leader William Seward and his allies declared their allegiance was to
a "higher law." In other words, the law was (or should be) whatever
Seward and his allies said it was (or should be) at the time. Under
Seward's Higher Law Theory, God Himself had to be a Radical
Republican. To Southerners, slaveholders or not, this was a direct
threat. In addition, the fact that they were demanding the tariff be
more than doubled only worsened the situation. The South, which
had less than 30 percent of the population, was already paying more
than 85 percent of the taxes, but Republicans wanted more. Dixie
leaders pleaded that such an increase would destroy the South economically. While mostly ignored, some abolitionist newspapers'
editorials blared that the South deserved economic crushing for its
sins. Southerners should pay because the North—especially New England—had a divine right to tariff income and could disperse it to railroads and banks as they chose. (Apparently, New England had had no
sins since the Salem Witch Trials.) Many Southerners remembered

Calhoun denouncing the tyranny of the majority and wished they had listened to him and seceded ten years before.

In those days, there was even less standardization of election days at the state and local levels than we have today. Elections happened throughout the year.[2] In 1860, the South watched in horror as the Republican party made significant gains in one Northern legislature after another. This trend may not have been in every case an endorsement of servile insurrection, but the South took it that way.

A dangerous situation was developing. The Democratic party was the traditional home of the South's non-slaveholding whites. The slaveholding oligarchy tended to support the conservative wing of the Whig party until it collapsed. The South reacted to the rise of the Republicans by becoming a one-party region. "Fire-eaters" such as Robert Barnwell Rhett of South Carolina, William L. Yancey of Alabama, Edmund Ruffin of Virginia, and John A. Quitman of Mississippi, joined the Democratic party and began urging separation as a way to put an end to Washington's political corruption and economic exploitation of the South. Despite their class differences, the small yeoman farmers now looked to the leaders of the slaveocracy for protection from the centralizing power of the greedy federal government.

The old guard establishment politicians of the South had to heed the demands of the fire-eaters or face political extinction. They had to embrace their demands that Southern principles and loyalty to the region took precedence over the political expediency of the past. No compromise was possible in this environment because the fire-eaters would not bargain or take one step back from their extreme positions, which had become widespread and explosive.[3] Even moderates like Jefferson Davis, for example, were now demanding laws that protected the South and would permit slavery in all of the territories, while allowing a tariff increase again was not even a consideration. The antebellum Washington establishment danced its last dance in 1860 in a troubled atmosphere. Everyone had a sense of foreboding.[4]

• • •

The Democratic party held its National Convention in Institute Hall in Charleston, South Carolina, in April 1860. Douglas was the frontrunner, but he had already mortally wounded his own candidacy. His "Freeport Doctrine" (i.e., his embrace of popular sovereignty) saved his credibility in the North and paved the way for his reelection to the Senate, but it had irredeemably discredited him with the fire-eaters. His break with the Buchanan administration over the Lecompton Constitution further undercut his tenuous support in the South. During a platform dispute, fifty-one Southern delegates walked out, led by William L. Yancey. They included all the delegates from Alabama, Florida, Georgia, Louisiana, Mississippi, South Carolina, and Texas, as well as three of Arkansas' four delegations and one delegate from Delaware.

There were six candidates for the nomination. Douglas received the majority but was fifty-six and a half votes short of the necessary two-thirds. By May 3, after fifty-seven ballots, he was still fifty-one and a half votes short. The convention was deadlocked.

The Democrats met again in the Front Street Theater in Baltimore on June 18. The fire-eaters put forth a resolution rejecting popular sovereignty and forcing slavery on the territories, whether they wanted it or not. It failed. Once again, the South walked out (or stayed away), only this time, it was 110 delegates. This total includes a scattering of New England Democrats, including convention chair Caleb Cushing, who opposed abolition, supported the Dred Scott Decision, and supported states' rights.[5] The rump convention nominated Douglas after two ballots.

Benjamin Fitzpatrick of Alabama was nominated for vice president, but he refused to accept it.[6] The nomination eventually went to former

U.S. senator and former governor Herschel V. Johnson of Georgia.[7] The moderate Democrats were hoping a Southern vice president would mollify the South, like John Tyler's acceptance of the vice presidential nomination in 1840 made it easier for Southerners to support William Henry Harrison. This time, however, the tactic did not work.

Ironically, had the South united behind the Douglas-Johnson ticket, Herschel Johnson might have become president, just as John Tyler did in 1841. Stephen Douglas died of typhoid fever and other maladies on June 3, 1861.

Immediately after the Baltimore walkout, a second Democratic convention met at Baltimore's Institute Hall. Presided over by Cushing, it adopted the pro-slavery platform rejected by Douglas' supporters and nominated John C. Breckinridge for president and Senator Joseph Lane of Oregon for vice president.

John C. Breckinridge (1821–1875), when he was a major general in the Confederate Army. *Courtesy of the American Battefield Trust*

With the Democrats in disarray, the Republican Party's National Convention met in Chicago in mid-May 1860. They sensed they had a good chance of winning. Seward was the leading contender, but his radicalism, open anti-Southern bigotry, and well-known lack of integrity worked against him. Abraham Lincoln was running second, followed by Salmon P. Chase of Ohio and Edward Bates of Missouri. Of the three,

Bates had little going for him except the backing of Horace Greeley and the powerful New York *Tribune*.

Except for Lincoln, the GOP candidates had serious political baggage. The Republicans also knew they would have to carry the West to win the election, and Lincoln was popular there. Greeley dropped the non-entity Bates and backed "Honest Abe," who secured the nomination on the third ballot.[8] The convention picked Senator Hannibal Hamlin of Maine as the vice presidential nominee. He brought geographical balance to the ticket, and, as a former Democrat, the GOP leaders hoped he could bring other anti-slavery Democrats into the fold.

The Republican platform did not change. It featured extremely high tariffs, no slavery in the territories, and subsidies for a transcontinental railroad that, of course, would go through the North, and that would exclude the South from any economic benefit of this massive, federal-supported, internal improvement.

The Constitutional Union Party nominated a fourth candidate. It had been formed from remnants of the defunct Know-Nothing and Whig Parties. It was a strict construction party and included Governor Sam Houston of Texas, Senator John J. Crittenden of Kentucky, and former senators John Bell of Tennessee, Edward Everett of Massachusetts, William A. Graham of North Carolina, and William C. Rives of Virginia. It met in the Eastside District Courthouse in Baltimore and nominated John Bell for president over Sam Houston in two ballots. Bell was a former Whig who opposed the Kansas-Nebraska Act and the Lecompton Constitution. Its vice presidential nominee was Edward Everett, another moderate. He was a former president of Harvard and secretary of state under Fillmore. The party's platform was "The Union as it is, the Constitution as it is." Bell argued that secession was unnecessary, but he ignored the tariff issue.[9] This ticket showed surprising strength, and it might have been better for the country if it had won, but it was a centrist party (like the Northern Democrats), and no centrist was going to win in 1860.

The election took place on November 6, 1860, and Lincoln received 1,865,908 votes or 39.8 percent of the total. He only needed 152 electoral

votes to win, however, and he carried eighteen states and garnered 180 electoral votes. Douglas and Northern Democrats received 1,380,202 votes (29.5
percent) but took only one state (Missouri). He also won three of New Jersey's
seven electors, giving him a total of twelve electoral votes. Breckinridge and
the Southern Democrats polled 848,019 votes (18.1 percent). They carried
eleven states worth seventy-two electoral votes. John Bell was not that far
behind with 590,901 votes (12.6 percent). He took three states and thirty-nine
electoral votes. A handful of splinter parties split the rest of the ballots.

The South viewed the election as a permanent shift of power. They had
had the presidency for forty-nine out of the seventy-two years it existed (more
than two-thirds of the time) and had played the most prominent role in
writing the Constitution, the Declaration of Independence, and the Bill of
Rights. They had supplied twenty-four of the thirty-six speakers of the
House and twenty of the thirty-five Supreme Court justices, giving them a
majority in the court always. Twenty-five of the thirty-six presidents *pro
tempore* of the Senate had been Southerners.[10] But they saw the end coming.
Demographics had finally weighed against them. As winter descended on
the country, their leaders were not only talking secession, they were selecting
meeting places and scheduling referendums to take action. Lincoln did not
help the situation by appointing at least two radicals to his cabinet: Seward
as secretary of state and Salmon P. Chase as secretary of the treasury.

Lincoln's top lieutenants, Salmon P. Chase and William Seward, secretary of the
treasury and secretary of state. *Courtesy of the Library of Congress*

Lincoln apologists have seized on the fact that four of the thirteen Confederate states made lengthy mention of slavery in their secession ordinances as one of their reasons for seceding. In a giant intellectual leap, they assert that this is "proof" that war was all about slavery. But three states (South Carolina, Texas, and Mississippi) mentioned the North's ignoring the law as a reason for leaving the Union—specifically the North's failure to extradite the John Brown raiders to Virginia as the law required. This fact is ignored by establishment historians. Apparently, it is insignificant when three states mention another factor in their secession, but another four states' mentioning slavery is overwhelming proof.

The Republicans also backed a territorial policy, which the Supreme Court had declared illegal when it issued the Dred Scott decision. Southerners concluded that they could not rely on the Republicans to respect, impartially enforce, or obey the law. They also realized that radicals now controlled federal patronage. They could and no doubt would assign abolitionists to public offices throughout the South. Some even feared (somewhat irrationally) that the national government might give such jobs to black men. Many more, however, worried the federal government might encourage or even instigate slave revolts.

"The South," Dr. Livingston wrote, "did not secede to protect slavery from a national plan of emancipation because no national political party proposed emancipation."[11] The states which mentioned slavery in their ordinances were reacting to the irresponsible attacks of the abolitionists and their embrace of terrorism and servile insurrection as legitimate means of gaining their objectives. The South feared (with considerable justification) that the Republican party was a revolutionary party that wanted to destroy the federation of states (as favored by Jefferson) in favor of a dominant central government funded by the South but controlled by the North. After Lincoln's election, Wendell Phillips, a leading abolitionist and Radical Republican, declared: "No man has a right to be surprised at this state of things. It is just what we have attempted to bring about. It is the first sectional party ever organized in this country.

It does not know its own face, and calls itself national; but it is not national—it is sectional. The Republican party is a party of the North pledged against the South."[12]

CHAPTER XI

THE REAL CAUSE OF THE WAR

The Northern onslaught upon slavery was no more than a piece of specious humbug designed to conceal its desire for economic control of the Southern states.

—Charles Dickens, 1862[1]

No soldier on either side gave a damn about the slaves.

—Shelby Foote, American historian[2]

For the love of money is the root of all evil....
1 Timothy 6:10

And now we come to the real cause of the war: money. Most wars have been about money or the transfer of riches and territory, which also equates to money, eventually. This economic factor should never be ignored.

Shortly after the Revolutionary War, the United States decided to transfer all state war debts to the federal government. This was a great benefit to the North. Their states were freed from their massive debts, now paid by the central government. The primary way the U.S. government had to raise funds was via tariffs, mostly from Southern resources. From the beginning, the South was footing the bulk of the expenses of the government. William Grayson, one of Virginia's first U.S. senators, warned that he was afraid that the South would become the "milch cow" of the Union.[3]

Grayson proved to be prophetic. Speaking in 1828, Thomas H. Benton (who opposed slavery) told the Senate: "Before the Revolution, iit [the

South] was the seat of wealth, as well as hospitality. Money, and all it commanded, abounded there. But how is it now? All this is reversed." "Why?" Benton rhetorically asked himself. Federal legislation was his answer. "Virginia, the two Carolinas, and Georgia may be said to defray three-fourths of the annual expense in supporting the Federal Government; and of this great sum, annually furnished by them, nothing, or next to nothing is returned to them, in the shape of Government expenditures." Benton went on to say: " ... the South must be exhausted of its money, and its property, by a course of legislation, which is forever taking away, and never returning anything. Every new tariff increases the force of this action. No tariff has ever yet included Virginia, the two Carolinas, and Georgia, except to increase the burdens imposed upon them."[4]

After seeing Senator Benton's remarks, the reader might well ask, "Why didn't the South leave the Union earlier than it did?" Part of it came close during the Nullification Crisis. Only after Henry Clay and John C. Calhoun reached their tariff reduction agreement in 1833 did South Carolina back off secession. For, despite the high tariff rates, the South and North both prospered then because they had a symbiotic economic relationship. When the Southerners bought their slaves from the Yankee flesh peddlers, they were using money loaned to them by Northern banks. The worldwide industrial revolution was based largely on textile manufacturing, which required enormous amounts of cotton. The South produced more than 75 percent of the world's cotton. The New England textile industry was built on this cotton, which was mostly planted, cultivated, picked, and ginned by slaves. Cotton, produced by slaves, built the North's prosperity like that of the Deep South. Even the Northern shipping industry depended on cotton and slavery. The North sent supplies (especially food and clothing) to the South via ship. These same vessels took back cotton (much of it produced by slaves) to the New England textile mills, of which there were thousands. They then used it to manufacture textiles, which they shipped abroad. As James Madison said, the road to profitable trade for New England ran through the cotton fields of the South.

Wall Street and the Northeastern banking industry also indirectly depended on cotton and slavery. Plantation owners often borrowed to buy new land and slaves, and New York banks were more than happy to loan money to them. Cotton was America's number one economic product, accounting for more than half of all exports.[5] The export value of cotton alone stood at $161,434,923 in 1859. That same year, the total value of all exports from the North stood at only $78,217,202.[6] In other words, the value of one Southern product accounted for more than twice the value of all Northern exports combined. As the country moved toward civil war in the late 1850s, the tax scales were tilted heavily against Dixie. President Buchanan told Congress: "The South had not had her share of money from the treasury, and unjust discrimination had been made against her.... "[7]

By 1860, 80 to 90 percent of federal revenue came from the Southern export trade, which was largely built on slavery. Leonard M. Scruggs, a distinguished author and historian, put the figure even higher, at around 95 percent.[8] Here we see the real reason Abraham Lincoln and the more moderate Republicans did not wish to disturb slavery in the South: from its establishment up until 1861, the United States government was mostly funded by Southern agriculture and especially the cotton industry, much of which depended on slave labor.[9] If slavery were abolished, federal funding would be eliminated with it. Thus, Lincoln and his allies only opposed the *expansion* of slavery into the territories. In doing so, Northern Republicans could create and then keep their lock on political power by adding more and more non-Southern states. The Southern states would become isolated and politically impotent vassal provinces and economic colonies, easily dominated and bullied by the more populous North, which would be in a position to pick their pockets whenever it wished.

Consider the Morrill Tariff as a prime example.

No sooner had the lower Tariff of 1857 passed than Northern elements in Congress began to agitate for its replacement. In 1858, Representative Justin Smith Morrill of Vermont introduced the Morrill Tariff in Congress. It would have raised the average dutiable *ad valorem* tax on imports from just under 20 percent in 1860 (under the Tariff of 1857) to more than 36 percent in 1862—and a whopping 47 percent within three years. Predictably, some of the protected Northern industries and corporations needed to import specific items, so these were classified as non-dutiable (not taxed).[10]

The South accounted for close to 82 percent of U.S. export business and for more than 83 percent of American tariff revenues even before the Morrill Tariff. About 80 percent of these revenues went to public works projects, railroads, and industrial subsidies in the North, enriching Northerners at the expense of the South.[11] The Morrill Tariff would make this unhealthy situation even worse. Despite its blatant unfairness, it passed the House of Representatives by a vote of one hundred five to sixty-four. Only one of the South's forty representatives voted for it.

The Morrill Tariff was—and protective tariffs in general are—particularly hard on exporters. By driving up the cost of imports, this tariff especially jeopardized the South's cotton market in Europe because England could develop new production regions in colonies such as India and lower the cost of imported cotton. The Southerners also faced retaliatory tariffs.

Congressman Thaddeus Stevens of Pennsylvania was one of the sponsors of the Morrill Tariff. He acknowledged that the bill would cause suffering in the South and West and would particularly hurt the poor, who would have to pay more for products, but it would benefit the Northeast through increased industrial production and the higher prices manufacturers could charge consumers.

Stevens was a radical abolitionist and an excellent speaker but not a nice person. He was profoundly anti-Southern and anti-Christian as well, once declaring that "the Bible is nothing but the obsolete history of a barbarous people."[12] He felt that if the South wanted to be prosperous, it should abolish slavery and become like the Northeast. That the South did not want to be like the Northeast was a fact that he simply could not understand, and he viewed it with malice.

Fortunately for the South, Robert M. T. Hunter of Virginia chaired the Senate Finance Committee. He bottled up Morrill's proposed tariff in committee so that it became an issue in the 1860 election campaign. Both Douglas and Breckinridge opposed high tariffs but not Lincoln. His support of the Morrill Tariff helped him carry the critical states of Pennsylvania and New Jersey by a plurality.

The Northern protectionists were pleased when the Deep South seceded and its senators went home. They had long wished to use the federal government to enrich themselves but had found their way blocked by the small government scruples of the Jeffersonian Constitutionalists. If the Northern industrial special interests could raise the tariffs on imports from Britain, they could sell Northern products at a higher price and thus reap higher profits. This is what Calhoun was trying to block when he demanded to know what business the government had picking the winners and losers in the private sector. But Jefferson was dead, Calhoun was dead, and Jefferson Davis had retired to his plantation on the Mississippi River. Now, the Northern protectionists could ram their tariffs through Congress without Southerners blocking them. Lincoln and his army could always force the South back into the Union later, if necessary. (At this time, of course, they had no idea what it would cost.) To do justice to the protectionists, they did not think force would be necessary. Many of them—Lincoln among them until April 4, 1861—thought the South was bluffing. Union general Donn Piatt recalled: "His views of human nature were low, but good-natured. This low estimate of humanity blinded him to the South. He could not believe that men would get up in their wrath and fight for an idea. He considered the movement South as a sort of political game of bluff, gotten up by politicians, and meant solely to frighten the North ... 'They [the Southern politicians] won't give up the offices,' I remember he said... "[13] (Lincoln's ambition in life was to hold high office, and he could not believe the Southern leaders would voluntarily give up their seats in the Senate and other high places.)

But the South was not bluffing.

The Morrill Tariff easily passed the House again, one hundred five to sixty-four. With the Deep South senators gone, Senator Hunter could no longer bottle it in committee. It passed the Senate twenty-five to fourteen. Because Lincoln and the Republican party had made the tariff's passage a major campaign issue and a test of party loyalty, Republican congressmen voted for it eighty-nine to two. In the Senate, Republicans voted for it twenty-four to zero. It is worth noting that the tariff bill had priority even before excluding slavery from the territories.[14] President Buchanan signed the tariff into law on March 2, 1861, two days before he left office.

For practical purposes, Henry Clay's America System was now the law of the land. It had been Lincoln's political North Star throughout his public career. But the America System, whatever its aims, only helped the North. The Constitution allowed the federal government to collect tariffs to fund itself, but it had never been meant to enrich some people at the expense of others. Now the Constitution was irrelevant. Turned on its ear, it no longer served as an instrument to limit federal power.

Justin S. Morrill (1810–1898), Congressman (1855–67) and U.S. Senator (1867–98) from Vermont. *Courtesy of the Library of Congress*

"The Morrill Tariff is a powerful and astonishing example of short-sighted partisans' greed and its catastrophic consequences," Leonard Scruggs wrote later.[15] The terms of the Morrill Tariff were so harsh that it virtually forced the rest of the South (Arkansas, Tennessee, North Carolina, and Virginia) out of the Union. Maryland, Kentucky, and Missouri might have left too, had they been allowed to do so.[16] After a forty-year history of economic abuse, the ties that bound the Union together disintegrated altogether. The Southern states which remained in the Union saw that they would be treated unfairly by the North. The Morrill Tariff, the North's refusal to enforce laws it didn't like, and open Northern sympathy with terrorists pushed the Southerners over the edge. Many who had been pro-Union before Harper's Ferry and the Morrill Tariff now favored secession.

● ● ●

There was a solution to the slavery problem, but it required recognition from all parties that it was a national problem that needed a national solution in which all parties sacrificed. All parties had profited from slavery. The irresponsible abolitionists only offered sacrifice from other people while most Northerners, many of whom had been more than willing to share in the profits associated with slavery directly and indirectly, were unwilling to share in any sacrifices. They were not willing to help pay for a compensated emancipation, for example. It's small wonder the Southern newspapers of the day editorialized about Northern hypocrisy.

Lincoln and his cronies had grand plans for the money they would get from their monstrously high tariffs. They did not believe the South was likely to go to war over this issue.

They were dead wrong.

Some Northern apologists tried to dismiss the Morrill Tariff as a cause for the war by pointing out that it had not passed the Senate before the South seceded. Author James Spence, however, addressed this issue in 1862 when he wrote: "The cotton States had indeed seceded previously, but why? Because, as we have seen, political power had passed into the hands of the North, and they anticipated from the change, an utter disregard of their interests, and a course of policy opposed to the spirit of the Constitution, and to their rights under it. Was it possible to offer the world more prompt or convincing proof than this tariff affords, that their apprehensions were well founded?"[17]

●　●　●

Some historians have questioned whether the South could have been a viable nation; however, the antebellum South was wealthier than many people today realize. Had it been an independent country in 1860, its economy would have been ranked the third largest on the European and American continents. Dixie had 33 percent of the nation's railroad mileage and was ahead of every other country in the world except, of course, the United States as a whole. It also had navigable rivers that did not freeze, several excellent ports, and a per capita income 10 percent higher than all the states west of Pennsylvania.[18] Its wealth was not confined to the affluent, planter class. It also had a large, highly industrious class of yeoman farmers. Most of them did not own slaves. Only about 6 to 7 percent of the Confederate enlistees had slaves. Slaveholding yeoman farmers usually had only one or two. They labored in the cotton fields right beside their chattels. But it is true that many were ambitious to own more. After all, the first masters who lived in the "Big House" were not born there. Most of them started out picking their own cotton.

Now that secession had come, most of the middle class in the Deep South looked toward the future with optimism. Now they would be able to keep more of their hard-earned income under a government that understood them better and was less exploitive and corrupt than that of the United States as a whole.

●　●　●

The Buchanan administration and Congress did not take any steps to coerce the South back into the Union for two reasons. First, they knew they had no constitutional right to do so. Second, the people of the North did not want them to return by a margin of about two to one.[19]

At first, the Northern newspapers were also ready to "let our erring brothers depart in peace." Horace Greeley, the editor of the *New-York Tribune*, wrote: "The South has as good a right to secede from the Union as the colonies had to secede from Great Britain."[20] "We must separate from them peacefully… " the *Albany Atlas and Argus* declared, and it went on to blame the Republicans for causing South Carolina's secession.[21] The pro-Lincoln *Indianapolis Daily Journal* said that "We are well rid of South Carolina… " and expressed gratitude to her for leaving. "If all the South follows her, let it."[22] The New York *Journal of Commerce* declared that it was time to stop assigning blame and to face facts: "… the Union [is] in fact already dissolved," it said, and it was time for Washington to adopt a policy of limiting secession, not to raise and arm men to butcher their friends in the South.[23] The *Detroit Free Press* wrote: "The people of these States, driven to desperation by the incessant warfare of abolitionism upon their most cherished rights, have withdrawn themselves from among us… " and Washington should recognize the Confederacy or go to war. The pro-Douglas newspaper hoped for peace, but, if there were a war, it said the blame would lie with the Republican party.[24] Even the *Northwest Daily Tribune*, a pro-Lincoln newspaper, said that if the South opted to form an independent nation, "they [would] have a clear moral right to do so."[25]

Only gradually did it occur to some of them what this would mean economically. A Manchester, New Hampshire, newspaper warned its readers: "The Southern Confederacy will not employ our ships or buy our goods. What is our shipping [worth] without it? Literally nothing. The transportation of cotton and its fabrics employs more ships than all other trade. It is very clear that the South gains by this process, and we lose. No—we MUST NOT 'let the South go.'"[26] The pro-Lincoln *New York Evening Post* pointed out on March 12, 1861, that if the government could not collect revenues from the seceded states, "the nation will become bankrupt."[27]

It was now clear that many of the Northern politicians had seriously miscalculated the depths of Southern feelings about the tariffs, Northern hypocrisy, disrespect for the rule of law, hate-filled abolitionist propaganda, slavery, protecting terrorists, encouraging servile insurrection, corporate welfare, cultural arrogance, and a host of other matters that provoked secession. The Southerners had, in fact, exercised their constitutional right to leave the Union, had formed their own government, and were now building their own army to defend it, if needed. But a successful Confederate States of America would also devastate the North economically. The new government in Montgomery, Alabama, enacted a tariff but set the maximum level at 10 percent. They felt that if 10 percent was good enough for God, it was good enough for them! Rather than pay the 47 percent duties for doing business in Northern ports, the countries of the world would prefer to pay 10 percent in New Orleans, Mobile, Savannah, Charleston, et al., and reap a huge dividend in the process. Many in the North now realized that the South must be cajoled or forced back into the Union if the North was not to face dire economic consequences. But how was that to be done? Abraham Lincoln, ever the calculating politician, had an answer.

CHAPTER XII

LINCOLN AND HIS AGENDA

His genius was little more than the lack of principle, which allowed no scruple to stand in the way of his design.[1]
—Caesar Borgia (Machiavelli's model)

We could have pursued no other course without dishonor; and as sad as the result have been, if it had all to be done over again, we should be compelled to act in precisely the same manner.
—Robert E. Lee

Inaugurated president of the United States on March 4, 1861, Abraham Lincoln arrived in Washington with a definite agenda, plain to anyone who had followed his career: more centralized government, more power to the chief executive, more money from the South to benefit the North and the West, and the prohibition of slavery in the territories to stop the spread of black people.

Thomas Landess, one of the scholars at the Abbeville Institute, wrote in 2015 that "all of us like the Lincoln whose face appears on the penny."[2] And indeed we do. He is the Lincoln of the myth: honest, kind, serious, dignified, firm in his principles and beliefs.

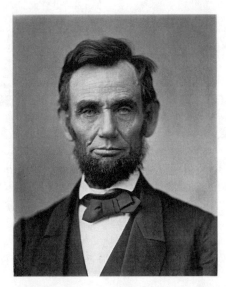

The Abraham Lincoln of the popular image. *Courtesy of Alexander Gardner, Mead Art Museum*

Unfortunately, this Lincoln never existed.

Abraham Lincoln is perhaps the most overrated man in American history. The real Lincoln was a reservoir of dirty jokes as well as Yankee stories. (The residents of the old Northwest did not consider themselves "Yankees" before the Civil War.) He had many humorous tales, anecdotes, yarns, and stories about the New England religious hypocrites and their dishonest peddlers. After the women had gone home and the children had been put to bed, men would gather around the stove at the local general store to enjoy "Honest Abe's" ribald humor and often obscene stories.[3] This is one reason parsons did not like him. Of the twenty-three preachers in his hometown of Springfield, Illinois, only three supported Lincoln in the presidential election of 1860.[4] (This was before the Johnson Amendment of 1954 gagged preachers and restricted their political freedoms.) Although Mrs. Mary Todd Lincoln claimed that he believed in the biblical Jesus, she admitted that he was not technically a Christian. Close personal friend and law partner William Herndon, however, rejected the idea that he was even a believer,[5] and Ward Hill Lamon declared that he "was not a Christian."[6] This fact, of course, did not prevent Honest Abe from memorizing many passages from the Holy Bible, such as "a house divided against itself cannot stand"[7] to quote to his devout constituents who were unaware that he was not a believer like many of them. Whether this made Lincoln a cynical politician, an astute one, or both depends on whose works you are reading.

Later, during the war, in areas occupied by the Union army, Union generals forced Southern preachers to pray for him. Failure to pray led to arrest, often by being dragged from the pulpit, and preachers were held in jail indefinitely, so Lincoln did receive support from the clergy, even if it was under duress.

Lincoln was the son of a shiftless farmer who lost most of his holdings due to poor land claims. He preferred uprooting his family and moving rather than settling down. Abe grew up in the wilderness around uneducated and often coarse men and women. He used foul language and lacked social graces. Through his own efforts, he mostly educated himself and was, in his own words, "a self-made man." He became a great public speaker and debater and was admitted to the bar, where he represented big corporations and big business against the little man. At various times, he represented the Illinois Central Railroad, the Chicago & Alton Railroad, the Ohio & Mississippi, and the Rock Island Railroad. Erastus Corning offered him the job of chief general counsel for the New York Central Railroad at $10,000 a year (about $265,000 in 2017 dollars), but Lincoln turned it down. He probably couldn't afford the pay cut.

Abraham Lincoln loved money and power. He and his minions openly admitted they wanted to remake America and "forge a new Union."[8] A typical cabinet appointee was Salmon P. Chase, his secretary of the treasury. In 1857, William D. Chadick of Alabama visited Ohio. He was searching for a home for a group of slaves liberated by the will of the late Samuel Townsend, and he thought Chase (then governor of Ohio) would be deeply interested in the project. On December 27, he met with him, and Chadick recalled Chase saying, "he would rather never see another free negro set his foot upon Ohio soil." Astonished, the Alabama man asked why. "Because their moral influence is degrading," Chase answered. Chadick pointed out the "glaring inconsistency" in him and other abolitionists, who wanted to free the slaves but did not want them living amongst them. "I do not wish to have the slave emancipated because I love him," the governor responded, "but because I hate his master."[9] This is the man Lincoln appointed secretary of the treasury and later chief justice of the United States Supreme Court.

Lincoln held white supremacist ideas throughout his life. Famously, during the Lincoln-Douglas debate at Charleston, Illinois, on September 18, 1858, he said: "I will say then that I am not, nor ever have been, in favor of bringing about, in any way, the social and political equality of the white and black races; that I am not, nor ever have been, in favor of making voters or jurors of negroes, nor of qualifying them to hold office, nor to inter-marry with white people; and I will say in addition to this that there is a physical difference between the white and black races which I believe will forever forbid the two races living together on terms of social and political equality."[10] General Piatt, a fervent abolitionist, recalled: "[Lincoln] could no more feel sympathy for that wretched race [Negroes] than he could for the horse he worked or the hog he killed."[11]

Abraham Lincoln was not idolized as some kind of godlike creature until after his death. Dr. James McPherson of Princeton later said, "Being assassinated when he was in a moment of victory made it possible to forget all of the criticism of him, the failures and the frustrations of the war years, and to see only the martyr." His life is now romanticized, though, as McPherson noted, he was "an often ruthless man."[12] Certainly, his contemporaries did not think very highly of him. Abolitionist Wendell Phillips called him "A huckster in politics... a first-rate second rate man."[13] General John C. Fremont said he had an "incapacity and selfishness, with disregard of personal rights, with violation of personal liberty and liberty of the press, with feebleness and want of principle."[14]

As Ward H. Lamon, the U.S. marshal and close personal friend chosen by Lincoln to accompany him to Washington, later wrote:

> ... the ceremony of Mr. Lincoln's apotheosis was not only planned and executed by men who were unfriendly to him while he lived, and that the deification took place with showy magnificence some time after the great man's lips were sealed in death. Men who had exhausted the resources of their skill and ingenuity in venomous detractions of the living Lincoln, especially during the last years of his life, were the first, when the assassin's bullet had closed the career... to undertake the self-imposed task of guarding his memory—not as a human being, but as a god.[15]

General Piatt recalled of Lincoln: "I saw a man of coarse, rough fiber, without culture."[16]

Edwin Stanton, later the brutal and ruthless Union secretary of war, met him in 1858 and took an instant dislike to him. Lincoln had been called in as a legal consultant on the McCormack Reaper patent infringement case. He called Lincoln a "giraffe" to his face and threatened to throw up his briefcase and leave if he joined the legal team. " ... he treated me so rudely I went out of the room," Lincoln recalled. McCormack appealed to Stanton, who replied: "I will not associate with such a damned gawky, long-armed ape!" Lincoln, who was in the next room, heard every word. When McCormack returned, Lincoln refunded his fee and left for home.

Stanton's dislike never abated. He often referred to the president as a "gorilla," an "orangutan," a "baboon," or a "low, cunning clown."[17]

Stanton was not the only one with a low opinion of Lincoln. This list was long and impressive. People who expressed dislike for him included Salmon P. Chase, Vice President Hannibal Hamlin, Secretary of State Seward, General Fremont, Senator Sumner, Senator Lyman Trumbell of Illinois, Senator Ben Wade of Ohio, Thaddeus Stevens, Senator Zack Chandler of Michigan, Henry Ward Beecher, Wendell Phillips, and Horace Greeley. On February 23, 1863, Richard H. Dana wrote to Thomas Lathrop: "... the lack of respect for the President in all parties is unconcealed... He has no admirers... "[18]

Five days after Lee surrendered, John Wilkes Booth shot Lincoln. While obviously not his intent, Booth immortalized Lincoln and saved him from an inevitable collision course with members of his own party regarding Southern "reconstruction." There is little doubt, given the way Republican leaders felt about him, they would have savaged him—assuming he did not flip-flop again. Only after his death on April 15, 1865, did these men jump on the Lincoln immortality bandwagon. Edwin Stanton was the first. "Now he belongs to the angels," he moaned seconds after Lincoln gave up the ghost. The press changed that remark to "Now he belongs to the ages." His life became romanticized and fictionalized. An old Confederate chaplain later remarked that Abraham Lincoln was unique among men because he became a Christian only after he died.[19] That Easter Sunday, many preachers throughout the North compared Lincoln to Jesus or Moses, who was allowed to see the Promised Land but not to enter it. But, as McPherson said, he was "an often ruthless man... " and certainly no biblical patriarch or messiah.[20]

Despite Democratic opposition and lack of support within his own party, President Lincoln had a long list of things he wished to achieve, and he barreled ahead. Items on his agenda included high tariffs; punitive taxation against the South to benefit other sections; mail subsidies to favored companies; land grants to railroads; bounties for New England fishermen; improvements to rivers and harbors, about 80 percent of them in the North; reserving coastal shipping for only U.S. (Northern) ships; exempting Northerners along the Canadian frontier from paying duties; refounding the nation by expanding and centralizing government power under the federal government; and creating what is called today an "Imperial Presidency." Lincoln wanted to become, and did become, the imperial ruler that Thomas Jefferson warned against in the Declaration of Independence. His first task, however, was to entice the Deep South back into the Union.

The Thirty-Sixth Congress met in December 1860, preoccupied with solving the secession crisis. In total, members of Congress introduced more than 200 resolutions aimed at solving or mitigating the situation, along with fifty-seven constitutional amendments. The three most serious attempts at the time to avoid disaster were the Southern peace commissioners, the Crittenden Compromise, and the Corwin Amendment.

The South sent three peace commissioners (Martin J. Crawford of Georgia, John Forsyth of Alabama, and Andre B. Roman of Louisiana) to Washington to negotiate its exit from the North and to avoid war, but Lincoln refused to meet or negotiate with them because it implied recognition of the Confederacy. Congress also proposed the Crittenden Compromise, but Lincoln refused to accept it because it restored the Missouri Compromise line (36 degrees 30 minutes), allowing slavery south of the line. This was contrary to the Republican platform, which would prohibit slavery in all territories.

The Corwin Amendment to the Constitution won traction.

In December 1860, President Buchanan asked Congress to set up a committee to draft an "explanatory amendment" vis-à-vis slavery. In the House, Thomas "Black Tom" Corwin of Ohio was chosen as the chairman. Corwin was a veteran politician who, at various times, was a state legislator, congressman, governor, U.S. senator, and congressman again. His amendment would forever prevent the federal government from interfering with slavery in the states where it existed. Corwin introduced it on February 27. President-elect Lincoln offered it quiet support. He also declared that, as president, he would not have the power to end slavery where it already existed. (He would later flip-flop on this statement as well.) The House approved it one hundred thirty-three to sixty-five on February 28, and the Senate adopted it on March 2 by a vote of twenty-four to twelve.[21] The amendment needed a two-thirds majority, so it barely squeaked by. Buchanan signed it later that day, two days before he left office.[22] It then went to the states for ratification. Kentucky, Ohio, Rhode Island, Maryland, and Illinois quickly ratified it. But the war would begin before any other states could approve it, making it moot.

Lincoln's support for the Corwin amendment disgusted some of the abolitionists, such as Lysander Spooner.[23] Spooner, a conspirator with John Brown, advocated violence and guerrilla warfare against the slave states.[24] He nevertheless wrote: "On the part of the North, the war was carried on, not to liberate the slaves, but by a government that had always perverted and violated the Constitution, to keep the slaves in bondage; and was still willing to do so, if the slaveholders could be thereby induced to stay in the Union."[25]

Spooner believed the government was a willing accomplice of the moneyed interests in the North. Their interest, he wrote, was "to monopolize the Southern markets, to maintain their industrial and commercial control over the South... "[26] These markets would, of course, be out of reach if the South seceded. After the war, Spooner wrote: "... these Northern manufacturers and merchants lent some of the profits of their former monopolies for the war, to secure to themselves the same, or greater, monopolies in the future. These—and not any love of liberty or justice—were the motives on which the money was lent by the North."[27]

Lincoln did not expect the Confederate States to embrace the Corwin Amendment, but he no doubt calculated that it might help keep the upper South (Tennessee, Missouri, Kentucky, North Carolina, Virginia, and Maryland) from seceding. He was right for a while.

● ● ●

The Deep South, however, did not take the bait. They had already seceded and were not interested in returning to the Union under any circumstance. Besides, the Corwin Amendment did not address the vital issues of tariffs and respect for the law. They had lost faith in the government of the United States. Robert E. Lee later said, "All that the South has ever desired was that the Union, as established by our forefathers, should be preserved; and that the government, as originally organized, should be administered in purity and truth." The South saw no chance of this happening under Lincoln and his myrmidons.[28]

After it was evident that the Corwin Amendment was not going to induce the Deep South (now the Confederate States of America) to return to the Union fold, it became clear to the president and his cronies that they had two choices: 1) let the Confederacy go in peace and deal with the ensuing economic disaster or 2) go to war with the South. It was also obvious that, for political reasons, Lincoln could not fire the first shot. It was calculated that Northern public opinion would be on the side of the South if that occurred, and Lincoln would not be able to wage a united war. From Lincoln's point of view, his agenda could only be secured if the South returned (or was forced) back into the Union, and this could only occur if the South started (or appeared to start) the war. Lincoln would have to maneuver the South into firing the first shot. The wily and manipulative trial and corporate attorney from Springfield was up to the task.

CHAPTER XIII

OVER THE EDGE

A lie doesn't become truth, wrong doesn't become right, and evil doesn't become good, just because it's accepted by a majority.
—Booker T. Washington

The Yankee repents of everyone's sin but his own.
—Daniel Harvey Hill, Confederate Lieutenant General and President of the University of Arkansas

Abraham Lincoln was elected president on Tuesday, November 6, 1860. The following day, there was great agitation in Charleston, and the Palmetto flag was raised instead of the Stars and Stripes. A federal officer tried to transfer supplies from the Charleston armory to the U.S. Army garrison at Fort Moultrie. City authorities arrested him. "So far as I am concerned," a judge told his court, "the Temple of Justice raised under the Constitution of the United States is now closed. If it shall never again be opened I thank God that its doors have been closed before its altar has been desecrated with the sacrifices of tyranny."[1] Throughout the North, abolitionists celebrated the Republican victory while meetings of an entirely different nature were held in the South, especially in South Carolina, which was again prepared to act.

South Carolina's legislature met in an unusual Saturday session on November 10. It passed an act calling for a secession convention to begin in Columbia on December 17. That same day, both U.S. senators from South Carolina resigned. This act sobered some Northerners. When business opened the following Monday, the financial markets in New

York City cratered. The next day, the South Carolina legislature voted to raise 10,000 volunteers for the defense of the state.

Throughout the nation, the great and small declared for or against secession, but in South Carolina, it was a one-sided decision. On December 20, by a vote of one hundred sixty-nine to zero, the convention opted to secede. It revoked its 1788 ratification of the U.S. Constitution.

Meanwhile, on December 10, six South Carolina congressmen and President Buchanan met to discuss the military situation in Charleston. Although he did not put it in writing, the president verbally pledged that if South Carolina did not attack the forts, the federal government would keep the status quo. He also promised to inform the state government of any change in policy immediately.

South Carolina accepted Buchanan's promise and pledged not to attack, a gentlemen's agreement, as it were, and therefore binding. They assumed that Major Robert Anderson's garrison at Fort Moultrie would remain there and not move to Fort Sumter. Buchanan, however, did not consider himself bound by his own words. The very next day, Major (later Major General) Don Carlos Buell, the representative of the War Department, met with Anderson in Charleston and told him that he had permission to abandon Fort Moultrie and transfer the garrison to Fort Sumter.[2]

Robert Anderson watched the deteriorating situation between Washington and Charleston with increasing dismay. He knew Fort Moultrie was indefensible. It faced Charleston Harbor, not the city, and private homes had been built nearly on top of it while livestock wandered in and out of the porous fort whenever they wished.

Knowing he lacked the manpower to defend Fort Moultrie, he quietly evacuated it on December 26, spiked his obsolete thirty-two-pounder guns, and took his men under cover of darkness to Fort Sumter, which was located on an uninhabited rock island in the middle of Charleston Harbor. He carried four months' supplies of provisions with him.[3] Fort Sumter was much easier to defend, but it also dominated the entrance to one of the South's most important harbors. The garrison would eventually have to be dealt with by South Carolina.

At the same time, a delegation from South Carolina arrived in Washington, D.C. Its purpose was to negotiate the removal of the garrison from Charleston waters and to obtain a peaceful settlement of all outstanding issues. Among other things, South Carolina was prepared to pay for its share of the public debt.

Anderson's act was looked upon as a provocation. In response, South Carolina forces took over the other harbor forts, including Moultrie and Castle Pinckney, on December 27. In marked contrast to the situation during the Nullification Crisis of 1833, the Deep South quickly expressed support for the insurgents. Alabama and Georgia even offered to send troops to Charleston.

Meanwhile, Northerners became frightened by their own handiwork. They had not believed the South would secede, but military companies began springing up all over the South and conducting drills in city parks and on the town squares. It was becoming evident that they were deadly serious and were not bluffing. "The Southern States were going farther than the [Northern] people had believed was possible," Senator Blaine recalled. "The wolf which had been so long used to scare, seemed at last to have come."[4]

In late 1860 and early 1861, Republican strength at the ballot box fell off remarkably in the municipal elections. Even in Boston, Wendell Phillips needed police protection to return home. Scheduled to speak in Philadelphia, Abolitionist leader George William Curtis was told by the Republican mayor that it would be extremely unwise to try. There would be a riot if he did. Lincoln had carried the city handily less than five weeks before.[5]

In Washington, D.C., President Buchanan met with the South Carolina commissioners on December 28, but only as a private citizen. The delegation insisted that Major Anderson and his garrison be withdrawn. Buchanan stalled and played for time. He refused to order

Anderson to return to Fort Moultrie, despite the recommendation of Secretary of War John B. Floyd.[6] Winfield Scott, the general-in-chief, wanted to reinforce Fort Sumter. Floyd declared that the government's refusal to put things back as they were "invited a collision."[7]

There were several cabinet meetings at the end of December 1860 and early January 1861. One of them became so heated that Floyd and acting Attorney General Edwin Stanton almost came to blows. Frustrated, Floyd resigned on December 29. The next day, South Carolina volunteers seized the Charleston Arsenal.

President-elect Lincoln, meanwhile, claimed that he "yearned" for peace but took absolutely no steps to secure it. He did not believe the situation was serious and still thought South Carolina was bluffing. Meanwhile, the U.S. government sent a transport, the *Star of the West*, to reinforce and re-provision Fort Sumter. The soldiers were hidden below deck, but the South Carolinians had been tipped off as to what was really happening by Secretary of the Interior Jacob Thompson of Mississippi.[8] On January 9, 1861, an artillery battery manned by cadets from the Citadel (South Carolina's military institute) fired on the ship and drove it off. Anderson continued to draw his supplies from the mainland of South Carolina, but he knew the secessionists could cut them off at any time.

Meanwhile, the rest of the Deep South seceded.

Referendums occurred, and legislatures and secession conventions met throughout the South in early 1861. On January 9, Mississippi voted to secede by a vote of eighty-four to fifteen. The next day, Florida voted sixty-two to seven to leave the Union. Alabama departed on January 11 by a vote of sixty-one to thirty-nine. Georgia seceded on January 19 after a vote of two hundred eight to eighty-nine. Louisiana left the Union on January 26 after a vote of one hundred thirteen to seven. Texas voted one hundred sixty-six to seven to secede on February 1. Governor Sam Houston tried to obstruct it and prevent Texas from joining the Confederacy. On March 16, he went to work and was shocked to find Lieutenant Governor

Edward Clark sitting at his desk. The secession convention had deposed him. Lincoln offered him 50,000 troops to keep Texas in the United States, but like Robert E. Lee, Houston did not care to remain in a union held together by bayonets. He declined the offer and retired.

The Convention of Seceded States met in Montgomery, Alabama, on February 4, 1861. On Friday, February 8, they adopted a constitution and created the Confederate States of America. The new constitution followed the U.S. Constitution, except that it outlawed the slave trade and allowed for the admission of non-slaveholding states. The issue of slavery was left to the individual states. In one area, it was vastly superior to the U.S. Constitution, then and now: it had a provision allowing a line-item veto.[9]

The Convention of Seceded States elected Jefferson Davis, a political moderate, provisional president on February 8 and recent anti-secessionist Alexander H. Stephens as vice president on February 9. The two men were not close and bickered. Stephens, however, was a good friend of Abraham Lincoln.

Davis was helping his wife trim the rose bushes at Brierfield, their plantation, when the dispatch announcing his election results arrived. Jefferson Davis turned pale. He had been expecting a general's appointment and, maybe, an assignment to command an army. There was no celebration at Brierfield that night. Unlike less astute or less experienced men, he saw beyond the momentary glory and public adulation to the immense difficulties and responsibilities that lay ahead.

The rest of the South did celebrate. They would now be free from the North's "endless insults" and "self-imposed ignorance" of their own history and responsibility vis-à-vis slavery.[10] Independence would also give the South more leverage in dealing with domestic terrorism, as advocated by Lysander Phillips, Thomas Wentworth Higginson, Samuel Gridley Howe, Theodore Park, Franklin B. Sanborn, Gerrit Smith, George Luther Stearns, and others.

Jefferson Davis (c. 1857) and his top general, Robert E. Lee. *Courtesy of the Library of Congress*

● ● ●

By March 1861, Northern public opinion was shifting. When the South first moved toward secession, the Northern press accepted it calmly. They agreed with General Scott, who said, "Let the wayward sisters go in peace."[11] But soon, Northern capitalists and politicians collared editors. They were told (accurately) that the free trade ports of New Orleans, Charleston, Savannah, and others would undercut the high duty ports of Boston, New York, Philadelphia, etc. They predicted that the North would lose at least half of its commerce. The Southern economy was prosperous, and the industrial, commercial, and financial classes of the North did not want it to slip beyond their grasp. Simultaneously, Lincoln was insisting that he must have his tariffs. The withdrawal of the South meant that the federal government lost more than 85 percent of its tax base. Also, an independent South with an economy based on free trade would be devastating competition for the North, which was addicted to the politically popular but morally corrupt and flawed "America System." Some Northern newspapers began advocating the use of military force to prevent this competitive situation.[12]

Abraham Lincoln, of course, appeared to support both sides. He spoke of how a house divided against itself could not stand and how the nation could not remain half slave and half free. From the other side of his mouth, however, he declared that he had no hostile intentions toward the South or slavery and offered to surrender forever any power the federal government might have to regulate the institution in states where it already existed. In other words, he was willing to leave the United States half slave, half free forever, or at least indefinitely. He also spoke of his great desire for peace while he prepared to trigger war. He still insisted on high tariffs.

● ● ●

It has been forgotten by today's Americans, but there were two potential flashpoints in the spring of 1861: Fort Sumter and Fort Pickens, the last located on Santa Rosa Island in Pensacola harbor, Florida. Santa Rosa Island was about forty miles long. Fort Pickens, on the west end, controlled the entrance to Pensacola, one of the best ports on the Gulf of Mexico.

In January 1861, Fort Pickens had a garrison inside the fort and a naval force outside it. They were outnumbered by Florida volunteers who held the town itself. Although Florida forces could have taken the fort, it would have started a war between the United States and the Republic of Florida. (The Confederate States of America did not yet exist.) Instead, Florida Senator Stephen Mallory made a deal with President Buchanan. The United States would not reinforce Fort Pickens, and the Florida (later Confederate) forces would not attack the fort. An armistice was agreed on January 29 and remained in effect until Lincoln broke the agreement in April. U.S. Captain Israel Vogdes of the First Artillery Regiment was the commander of a Union force aboard the USS *Brooklyn*. He and his men were supposed to reinforce the fort but stopped at the Pensacola sandbar. When he learned of the armistice, Vogdes returned to his vessel.

The stalemate continued until March 12 when, at Lincoln's command, General Scott sent Captain Vogdes an order: "At the first favorable moment, you will land your company, reinforce Fort Pickens, and hold the same until further orders."[13] This order was in direct violation of the armistice of January 29 and was an act of war—issued only eight days after Honest Abe became president.

Captain Vogdes did not receive the order until March 31. He requested Captain Henry A. Adams,[14] the commander of the frigate USS *Sabine* and the other ships in the Pensacola area, to provide him with the boats and support necessary to carry out this directive.[15] Adams realized that acting on this command would start a war, so he refused to recognize it because it came from an army general and contradicted his last standing orders from Isaac Toucey, Buchanan's secretary of the navy, which were to avoid war. He wrote to Secretary of the Navy Gideon Welles: "I can not take on myself under such insufficient authority as General Scott's order to the fearful responsibility of an act which seems to render civil war inevitable... "[16] "Captain Adams averted open war on April 1, 1861, by refusing to obey this order," Huger W. Johnstone wrote later.[17] In his report to the secretary of the navy, Adams said: "It would be considered not only a declaration but an act of war, and would be resisted to the utmost."[18]

Adams also reported that, "At present both sides are faithfully observing the agreement [armistice] entered into by the U.S. Government and Mr. [Stephen] Mallory[19] and Colonel [William Henry] Chase.[20] This agreement binds us not to reinforce Fort Pickens unless it shall be attacked or threatened. It binds them not to attack it unless we attempt to reinforce it."[21]

Apparently, Captain Adams thought Welles did not understand the true situation at Pensacola and did not want to start a war. It did not occur to him that starting a war was exactly what Welles wanted to do. The secretary was not happy when he received Adams's dispatch. On April 6, Welles responded to the captain and made it clear that he and the administration wanted war. He sent the forty-seven-year naval veteran what amounted to a letter of reprimand. "Your dispatch of April 1 is received," he wrote. "The Department regrets that you did not comply with the request of Capt. Vogdes. You will immediately on the first favorable opportunity after receipt of this order, afford every facility to Capt. Vogdes to enable him to land the troops under his command, it being the wish and intention of the Navy Department to co-operate with the War Department, in that object."[22]

In the meantime, in Washington, D.C., on February 6, Lincoln's agent, Gustavus V. Fox,[23] met with Lieutenant Norman J. Hall, who was sent from Fort Sumter by Major Anderson. They discussed relieving the fort.[24] They had several more conferences over the next few days on the same topic, and Fox wrote General Scott on March 8, informing him that Hall was bringing the relief plans to Major Anderson if the Rebels would let him back into the fort. The Lincoln administration (including, among others, Lincoln, Fox, Hall, and Montgomery Blair, the newly designated postmaster general)[25] was clearly scheming to relieve Fort Sumter before February 6, and these plans were well advanced by Inauguration Day.[26] The correspondence suggests that the president-elect thought that Southern secession was little more than posturing. A little show of force would resolve the problem. It was the first of many costly mistakes he would make over the next four years.

Meanwhile, Lincoln delivered his inaugural address on March 4, 1861. One author called it his "slavery forever" speech.[27] The Trenton *Daily True American* called it ambiguous. He spoke of enforcing the laws, for example, but only "as far as practicable." Much of it was vague.[28] No one knew what Lincoln intended to do.

Lincoln, Blair, Fox, and Scott met for the first of several conferences on March 13. General Scott was opposed to war,[29] so he was mostly kept "out of the loop" in March and April 1861.

Major Robert Anderson, May 1861. *Courtesy of the Library of Congress*

Stephen A. Douglas gave a rousing speech to the Senate on March 15. He called for peace and introduced a resolution calling for the withdrawal of all U.S. forces from Confederate territory, except for Key West and Tortugas, isolated islands off the Florida coast, which he considered international in scope. It was understood at that time, and assurances were given to the Confederate commissioners, that Fort Sumter was to be evacuated soon, if not sooner.[30]

U.S. Supreme Court Justice John Campbell was acting as an intermediary between the Confederate commissioners and the new Secretary of State, William H. Seward. Seward assured Campbell more than once that Fort Sumter would be evacuated. On March 15, he promised that "Sumter will be evacuated in ten days."[31] Campbell met with Seward again five days later. This time, he brought Samuel Nelson, also a Supreme Court justice, with him, as a presumed witness, for Seward was not known for his honesty. Once again, however, the secretary of state promised that Sumter was going to be evacuated. Author Huger William Johnstone recorded that Seward again assured the two justices that the Lincoln administration had no intention of reinforcing Sumter and would inform Campbell if it decided to alter the status of Fort Pickens.[32] Johnstone noted that he was quoting Judges Campbell and Nelson, "whose veracity, unlike Seward's, has never been questioned."[33]

Seward was lying again. The plan was for him to distract and stall
the Rebel commissioners until Fort Sumter could be reinforced. Lincoln's
emissary Fox, left Washington on March 19 and met with Major Anderson on the twenty-first. They decided that the garrison would hold out
until April 15.[34] Lincoln was personally involved by March 29. He sent
a dispatch to Secretary of the Navy Gideon Welles, saying, "I desire that
an expedition, to move by sea be got ready to sail as early as the 6th of
April ... " His memo called for three ships of war (the *Pocahontas*, the
Pawnee, and the *Harriet Lane*) to enter Confederate territorial waters,
carrying 200 reinforcements with one year's stores.[35] Two days later,
Seward once again assured Campbell that Lincoln would not supply Fort
Sumter and had no desire to reinforce it.[36]

In early April, David D. Porter, captain of the *Powhatan,* and a few
other ships sailed for Pensacola. Porter's orders were to place himself
in the harbor at Pensacola. He was delayed by gales and would not
arrive until April 17. Another task force under Commander Stephen
Rowan was also sent to Charleston on April 9. He sailed from Hampton
Roads, Virginia, with the USS *Pawnee* and the Revenue Cutter *Harriett
Lane.*[37]

On April 2, General Scott sent a remarkable order, dated April 1, to
Brevet Colonel Harvey Brown at Fort McHenry, Maryland:

> You have been designated to take command of an expedition
> to reinforce and hold Fort Pickens, in the harbor of Pensac-
> ola... You will proceed to New York, where steam transpor-
> tation for four companies will be engaged, and, putting on
> board such supplies as you can ship, without delay proceed
> at once to your destination.... The object and destination of
> this expedition will be communicated to no one to whom it
> is not already known.
>   (Signed) Winfield Scott
>   Approved April 2nd, 1861
>   (Signed) Abraham Lincoln[38]

Fort Pickens, Florida. *Courtesy of* Harper's Weekly, *February 23, 1861*

Presidents do not ordinarily approve orders like this from generals, but Scott knew it would violate the truce with the Confederates, who would undoubtedly fire on the ships and inaugurate civil war. It is obvious that he needed or wanted Lincoln's co-signature before he committed an act of war. He wanted future generations to know that the decision to go to war was Lincoln's, not his. Lincoln not only signed the order, but he also issued a second order (also dated April 1) to "All officers of the Army and Navy" to aide Brown and co-operate with him as needed. The president signed this order himself.[39]

There were now five military expeditions in, steaming toward, or about to sail for Southern territorial waters:

1) the Welles-Fox Expedition, heading for Charleston;
2) the Rowan Expedition, also heading for Charleston;
3) Captain Adams' ships, lurking off Santa Rosa Island;
4) Colonel Brown's Expedition, heading for Pensacola; and
5) Porter's Expedition, also steaming for Pensacola.

● ● ●

In the meantime, the Virginia Convention was alarmed that Lincoln's inaugural address had in it hints of coercion and usurpation of power, that Lincoln had rejected the Crittenden Compromise, and that he refused to meet with the Confederate peace delegation sent by President Davis. The convention decided to send a peace commission of its own to Washington. Instructed to meet with Lincoln, it was to learn his views and express to him their apprehensions. It consisted of William B. Preston, Alexander H. H. Stuart, and George W. Randolph. They were Union men but only conditionally so. "If our voices and votes are to be exerted farther to hold Virginia in the Union, we must know what the nature of that Union is to be … " Mr. Preston declared. "If the power of the United States is to be perverted to invade the rights of States and of the people, we would support the Federal Government no farther."[40]

On April 2, the very day Lincoln approved a secret act of war, "Honest Abe" asked Seward to send Allan B. Magruder, the judge advocate of the U.S. Naval Court, and instructed him to go to Richmond where he was to confer with Alexander Stuart, Judge George W. Summers (a highly respected member of the Virginia Convention and a solid Union man), and convention president John Janney. Magruder told the Virginians that he was authorized by Seward to inform them that Fort Sumter would be evacuated on Friday of the following week.[41]

Magruder said that Seward had asked Judge George William Summers, Janney, or Alexander H. H. Stuart to come to the White House for a secret meeting but, if they could not, to send another strong Unionist. Janney and Stuart (and apparently Summers as well) did not feel they could go without being recognized, so they sent Colonel John B. Baldwin instead.[42] It was obvious that Abraham Lincoln had asked for this meeting or at least had consented to it.

Baldwin was more or less smuggled into Washington. He arrived in the nation's capital early in the morning and was driven to the home of Magruder's brother, Captain John B. Magruder, the future Confederate general, where he ate breakfast. Allan Magruder then conducted him by carriage (with windows carefully covered) to Seward, who took him to the White House.

Shortly after nine o'clock a.m. on Thursday, April 4, Colonel Baldwin stood at a door of the White House. The porter agreed to inform Lincoln that he was there but told him there was no hope of his the seeing the president because he was already conferring with several important visitors. The porter returned with a surprised look on his face and told the guards to admit Baldwin at once.

Lincoln was in his business room, consulting with three or four elderly men. When Seward whispered in his ear, Lincoln stood up and abruptly ended the meeting. He escorted Baldwin upstairs to a private bedroom and closed and locked the door. The president sat on the bed and asked the colonel about the true sentiments of the majority of the Virginia Convention delegates. He spat on the carpet from time to time throughout the interview.

Baldwin told him that Virginia would stay in the Union if the new administration respected the Constitution and did not abrogate the rights of any state. This would have included taking military action against the cotton states.

Colonel John Brown Baldwin, who conferred with Abraham Lincoln in an unsuccessful attempt to prevent war. *Courtesy of Anderson Studio, Richmond, Virginia Historical Society*

The answer did not please the tall man from Illinois. "Yes," he said, "your Virginia people are good Unionists, but it is always with an *if*! I don't like that sort of Unionism."[43]

Baldwin respectfully but firmly explained that, in one sense, all free men could only be conditional Union men. When Unionism treated groups or sections of people unequally, the benefit of the Constitution was lost, and "Union" might become another name for mischievous oppression. Although Virginia voted against Lincoln, Baldwin said, she would treat him as if he were their first choice—provided he adhered faithfully to the laws and the Constitution. In return, Virginia would do all she could to keep the border states in the Union. Secession, however, was a constitutional right, and Virginians did not believe the federal government had any right to coerce a state by force of arms.

Lincoln continued not to like what he was hearing . He said that his advisors had assured him that all the speeches and resolutions from the Deep South were just "a game of brag." The Southern position had "nothing in it but talk."[44]

The Virginian assured Lincoln that he fatally misunderstood the South.

Suddenly Lincoln's eyes opened to the truth. He slid off the edge of the bed and began nervously pacing back and forth. "I ought to have known this sooner!" he snapped, clearly perplexed. "You are too late, sir, too late! Why did you not come here four days ago, and tell me all this!?" There was a look of fury on the chief executive's face. He was now pacing furiously and grasping his hair as if he were about to pull it out by the roots. He was obviously highly agitated.

Baldwin tried to explain that he had come as fast as he could, as soon as he learned that Lincoln again wanted his advice, but the president was beside himself.

"Yes, but you are too late, I tell you, *too late*!"[45]

Baldwin took this to mean that coercion had been decided on within the last four days. Unlike Baldwin, Lincoln knew that there were four war expeditions already sailing south.[46]

Lincoln's advisors had convinced him that their fear of servile insurrection would paralyze the South and the best way to solidify the Republican triumph at the polls was to force a confrontation. The South, they said, would back down.

But the South didn't.

Baldwin suggested the president call a conference of the states and to issue a "peaceful union proclamation." This, he said, would paralyze the secession movement.

Colonel Robert Dabney, D.D., recalled that "the policy urged by Colonel Baldwin would have disappointed the hopes of legislative plunder, by means of inflated tariffs, which were the real aims for which free-soil was the mask."[47]

Now Lincoln came to the point. He appealed to the Virginia Unionist to adjourn the Virginia Convention *sine die.* The convention had considered secession resolutions three times and had rejected the idea three times by votes of three to one but was still in session. It was taking a "wait and see" attitude. Both men knew that, if Virginia joined the Deep South, she would add a vast amount of military muscle and brains to the C.S.A. She also had a great deal of influence. If Virginia seceded, the rest of the Upper South was likely to follow; but if the Convention adjourned permanently, Virginia would not secede nor the upper South with it.

Baldwin rejected the idea out of hand. He sensed that Lincoln wanted war and tried to persuade him to let the South go peacefully. He pointed out the historical and economic ties it had to the North and predicted that they would eventually lead the Southern states back into the Union. Lincoln responded: "And open Charleston, etc., as ports of entry with their 10% tariff? What, then, would become of my tariff?"[48]

Startled by his interview with Colonel Baldwin, Lincoln knew that war, made inevitable by his actions, was about to start. But until this meeting, he did not think Virginia would leave and join the fight. Lincoln had badly miscalculated. Enemy territory would now be just across the Potomac River, and what would happen if Maryland to his north joined the Rebels? Thinking ahead, this would have contributed to his agitation that morning; but it was too late now—unless he openly backed down.

But, as Reverend Dabney wrote later, "he had not manliness enough to recede."[49]

For his part, Colonel Baldwin was disappointed in Lincoln. Until that morning, he had not thought Lincoln capable of such duplicity. When he left the White House, he realized that Lincoln's purpose in calling the meeting was not peace but to get the convention to adjourn. This would make it easier for the North to win the war by keeping Virginia from seceding with the other border states.[50]

The editorial writer for the *New York Herald* also could see through Lincoln. On April 5, he wrote: "We have no doubt Mr. Lincoln wants [President Davis] to take the initiative in capturing... forts in its waters, for it would give him the opportunity of throwing [to the South] the responsibility of commencing hostilities."[51]

●●●

Welles sent his order to Captain Adams via a special messenger, Lieutenant J. L. Worden, USN, who traveled by rail from Washington to Richmond to Augusta to Atlanta. In the heart of Confederate territory, he became understandably nervous. He read the dispatches (which were dynamite), committed them to memory, and burned them. This act, more than likely, saved his life.

Worden arrived in Pensacola about midnight on April 10. The next day, he met with Braxton Bragg, the Rebel commander in the Pensacola area and assured him he had a verbal message of a "pacific" nature for Captain Adams. Bragg decided to let him proceed and visit the Union skipper. The weather, however, was so bad that Worden could not reach Adams's ship until April 12. That night, taking advantage of the limited visibility, Vogdes reinforced the fort under cover of darkness with a mixed marine/army battle group.

After Worden delivered his message, he returned to Pensacola. He avoided seeing General Bragg again and instead boarded a train for Montgomery. He arrived in the Alabama capital on the morning of April

13, where Confederate authorities arrested him. By now, Rebel forces had fired on Fort Sumter, and Bragg knew that the message he had carried to Captain Adams was not "pacific." Fortunately for him, the Southerners decided to hold him as a prisoner-of-war, not as a spy. Worden would later command the USS *Monitor* in her epic battle with the Confederate ironclad *Merrimac*.

• • •

Meanwhile, events in Charleston raced to their conclusion.

Jefferson Davis, Governor Francis W. Pickens of South Carolina, and Confederate brigadier general P. G. T. Beauregard, the commander of Southern forces in Charleston, had about enough of Abraham Lincoln's subterfuges. They were no fools, and they realized Lincoln and Seward were playing for time so that they could get their military forces in position to reinforce Forts Sumter and Pickens. The question now was this: would they let them get away with it?

Author James H. Street wrote that "No one seriously thought the Confederacy long would tolerate a 'foreign' garrison at the mouth of Charleston harbor. It was something like a Southern garrison on Governor's Island in New York harbor."[52] Charleston was the most important Southern port between Norfolk and New Orleans. By now, the naturally irascible Davis had concluded that Lincoln was looking for a war and would eventually find a pretext. He decided that the showdown might as well come at Charleston.

Lincoln presently had five war expeditions in Southern waters or preparing to enter them. Even so, on April 7, Lincoln's crony, Secretary of State Seward, wrote Judge Campbell and assured him of his pledges concerning the evacuation of Fort Sumter. Imagine the judge's dismay when he opened his morning paper the next day and read: "An authorized messenger from President Lincoln informed Governor Pickens and General Beauregard that provisions will be sent to Fort Sumter—peacefully, or otherwise by force."[53]

That the Lincoln administration was engaged in "'systematic duplicity' is clearly apparent to any candid mind," Huger William Johnstone concluded.[54] On Monday, April 8, the Confederacy cut off Fort Sumter's mail and its supply of food and other provisions.[55]

Shortly after that, the Confederates intercepted a letter from Major Anderson. He questioned the strategic importance of the fort but concluded: "We shall strive to do our duty, though... my heart is not in the war which I see is to be thus commenced."[56]

Anderson followed his instructions from Washington and refused to surrender. He met with Southern envoys and told them that he would have to capitulate on April 15, if they would only wait. But the Rebels saw through this in a heartbeat. By April 15, Fort Sumter would be reinforced and Anderson would no doubt have new orders—which would not include surrendering on April 15.

The Fox expedition sailed from New York City on the morning of Tuesday, April 10. It ran into a gale and was dispersed. When the main vessel, the steamer *Baltic*, arrived at 3:00 a.m. on April 12, only the *Harriett Lane* was there to greet it. Commander Rowan in the *Pawnee* arrived at 7:00 a.m., but the main combat vessel, the *Powhatan*, was a no-show. Only later did Fox learn that it had been ordered to Pensacola on April 7.

Without the *Powhatan*, the U.S. naval forces were of no use in the Battle of Fort Sumter, which they watched from offshore. General Beauregard opened fire on the fort at 4:00 a.m. on April 12. (It is one of history's minor ironies that Major Anderson was Beauregard's favorite instructor when he was a cadet at West Point.)

Anderson had forty-eight guns and eighty-five soldiers, as well as help from some of the forty-three workmen employed in the fort. Beauregard had about seventy guns and more than 4,000 men. Although the Federals' deficit was less than two to one in cannons, the fight was much more lopsided than that would indicate because Anderson's supply of ammunition was severely limited. The bombardment lasted thirty-four hours. Fort Sumter hauled down its flag on April 13. The fort was severely battered but, remarkably, there were no casualties. The formal surrender took place on April 14. Four days later, Anderson wrote to Secretary of War Simon Cameron:

> Having defended Fort Sumter for thirty-four hours, until the quarters were entirely burned, the main gates destroyed by fire, the gorge walls closed from the effects of the heat, four barrels and three cartridges of powder only being available, and no provisions remaining but pork, I accepted the terms of evacuation offered by General Beauregard, being the same offered by him on the 11th instant, prior to the commencement of hostilities, and marched out of the fort Sunday afternoon the 14th instant, with colors flying and drums beating, bringing away company and private property, and saluting my flag with fifty guns.
>
> Robert Anderson
>
> Major, 1st Artillery, Commanding.[57]

On Monday, April 15, Abraham Lincoln issued a proclamation declaring that an insurrection had begun and called for 75,000 volunteers to suppress the "rebellion." This would be the largest military force ever assembled on the North American continent to that date. Congress was out of session at the time, so he called a special session for July 4. He could have had them assembled in ten days, but this did not fit his agenda. He chose for them to meet in three months because, he believed, he could defeat the South by then.

Meanwhile, the Virginia Peace Commission arrived in Washington on Friday, April 12, and promptly headed for the White House. They were told to come back the next day, although Lincoln did meet with them briefly. They sat down again on April 13 while the guns were firing on Fort Sumter. Alex Stuart took the lead and urged forbearance and called for the evacuation of Forts Sumter and Pickens. Lincoln objected because all the goods from Europe would be imported through the ports of Charleston, etc., and his sources of revenue would dry up. "If I do that, what will become of my revenue? I might as well shut up house-keeping at once!" he exclaimed to Stuart.[58] Then he gave Stuart and the other commissioners assurances that he wanted peace. Seward and Attorney General Bates chimed in and echoed the president.

Of Lincoln's April 15 proclamation, economic historian Jeffery Rogers Hummel wrote: "At a single stroke of the pen, Lincoln had more than doubled the Confederacy's white population and material resources."[59] The Virginia Commission was back in Richmond by then. Stuart opened his newspaper at breakfast at the Exchange Hotel and read about Lincoln's call for troops. "I thought it must be a mischievous hoax," he recalled, "for I could not believe Lincoln guilty of such duplicity." He sent Seward a telegram at once, asking if it were genuine. Then other newspapers arrived, confirming that it was.[60]

Alexander H. H. Stuart, former secretary of the interior and law partner of Colonel John B. Baldwin. A Virginia Unionist, he tried unsuccessfully to negotiate peace between the United States and the Confederate States of America. *Courtesy of the U.S. War College*

There was a federal order to Virginia to supply five regiments for the Union Army. Governor John Letcher wrote back to US Secretary of War Simon Cameron on April 16: "You have chosen to inaugurate civil war, and having done so, we will meet it in a spirit as determined as the [Lincoln] Administration has exhibited toward the South."[61]

The next day, the Virginia Convention voted 85 to 55 to secede. Both Colonel Baldwin and Judge Summers cast ballots against leaving the Union. The Old Dominion State was followed by Arkansas (May 6); North Carolina (May 20); and Tennessee (June 8).

A few days after Lincoln called for volunteers, a Northern politician wrote to Colonel Baldwin and asked what the Union men in Virginia would do now. Baldwin replied, "There are now no Union men in Virginia."[62] Virginia put the issue of secession to a popular vote on May 23. It passed, 96,750 to 32,134.[63]

Except for a handful of areas such as east Tennessee, the South was now united in war, but so was the North. It was clear that Abraham Lincoln's duplicity had worked. He had outmaneuvered Jefferson Davis diplomatically and had manipulated him into firing the first shot. Huger William Johnstone later commented that it was said of Caesar Borgia (Machiavelli's model), "His genius was little more than the lack of principle, which allowed no scruple to stand in the way of his design."[64] The Northern public, unaware of what had happened behind the scenes, united behind the flag, just as Lincoln thought they would. Old Glory was fired on! It was time to forget political differences and rally behind the colors! Also, the average Northerner's desire to preserve the Union ran more deeply than a lot of Rebels thought. Many Southerners could not believe that the Northern volunteers were willing to risk their lives to keep unwilling partners in the Union—but they were. President Davis made a serious miscalculation when he ordered his batteries to fire on Fort Sumter. He awakened a sleeping giant, and there would be hell to pay.

Fort Sumter, April 1861, after the Confederates occupied it. Note the Confederate flag. *Courtesy of Alma A. Pelot, National Archives*

But was the Confederacy responsible for the start of the Civil War? After all, it did fire the first shot.

At 6:37 a.m. on the morning of December 7, 1941, the USS *Ward*, a 1,267-ton destroyer, spotted a Japanese submarine trying to sneak into Pearl Harbor. She attacked it with her main battle guns and depth charges and sank it. These were the first shots fired in the Battle of Pearl Harbor. The Japanese did not attack the U.S. naval base until 7:48 a.m.

Did the United States start World War II? After all, she did fire the first shot.

The answer to such rhetorical questions is, of course, "No." In each case, the aggressor did not literally fire the first shot, although they did plan for war and decided to launch aggressive actions, such as violating the territorial waters of their foe; however, as Churchill wrote, the victor writes the history.[65] In the court of public opinion, shaped by years of Northern propaganda, the C.S.A. bears sole responsibility for starting the war. This author, for one, doesn't belief the South deserves this stigma. The reader, of course, must draw his or her own conclusions.

Abraham Lincoln, meanwhile, was pleased with how things had turned out but was concerned that his friend, G. V. Fox, was depressed that his Fort Sumter mission had failed. On May 1, Lincoln wrote him a letter saying that the administration got what it wanted. "I sincerely regret that the failure of the late attempt to provision Fort Sumter should be the source of any annoyance to you ... " the president wrote. He continued,

> You and I both anticipated that the cause of the country would be advanced by making the attempt to provision Fort Sumter, even if it should fail; and it is no small consolation now to feel that our anticipation is justified by the result."
>
> Very truly, your friend,
> A. Lincoln[66]

In the meantime, people who opposed Lincoln's war were arrested all over the North. One of them was Francis Key Howard, a grandson of Francis Scott Key, the author of "The Star-Spangled Banner." Ironically, he was incarcerated in Fort McHenry, Maryland. He wrote: "When I looked out ... I could not help being struck by an odd, and not pleasant coincidence. On that day, forty-seven years before, my grandfather, Mr. F. S. Key, then a prisoner on a British ship, had witnessed the bombardment of Fort M'Henry. When, on the following morning, the hostile fleet drew off, defeated, he wrote the song so long popular throughout the country, 'The Star-spangled Banner' ... The flag which he had then so proudly hailed, I saw waving in the same place, over the victims of as vulgar and brutal a despotism as modern times have witnessed."[67]

CHAPTER XIV

TYRANNY AND EMANCIPATION

Slavery is no more the cause of this war than gold is the cause of robbery.[1]
—Joel Parker, Governor of New Jersey (1863–66; 1871–74)

The sight of the Confederate battle flag always reminded me of the immense bravery of the soldiers who served under it.
—Union General Joshua Chamberlain

As soon as the Republicans got control of Congress in early 1861, they took full advantage of their majority. First, they passed the highest tax on imports in American history (the Morrill Tariff). They set up a national banking system under which favored institutions were basically entitled to create money and control the currency and credit of the United States.[2] They launched a massive giveaway of federal lands, some to homesteaders, but most to railroads and mining interests. None of it went to African Americans. They set up a contract labor law, which came close to enslaving gangs of foreign workers and depressed the wages of U.S. workers, further enriching the Republican fat cats on Wall Street and various corporate headquarters throughout the North. They also passed another Morrill Act for "land grant" colleges, opening the door for federal involvement in education for the first time. It was clear that the first sectional party intended to remake America into an image of the party's own choosing.

Meanwhile, the South prepared for war. The threat of military invasion does not mean much to modern-day Americans since they have never had to face the threat of one, but it meant a great deal to Southerners in

155

1861. The Reverend A. D. Betts of North Carolina, for example, wrote: "One day in April, 1861, I heard that President Lincoln had called on the State troops to force the seceding States back into the Union. This was one of the saddest days of my life. I had prayed and hoped that war might be averted. I had loved the Union and clung to it. That day I saw war was inevitable. The inevitable must be met. That day I walked up and down my porch in Smithville [now Southport, N.C.] and wept and suffered and prayed for the South."[3] After he finished crying, Reverend Betts joined his local military company, which became part of the Thirtieth North Carolina Infantry. It started out with about 900 men. When it surrendered at Appomattox four years later, it had 153 men.

So it was throughout the South. Patrick Cleburne, who was originally from Ireland but who settled in Helena, Arkansas, wrote: "I am with the South in death, in victory or defeat. I believe the North is about to wage a brutal and unholy war on a people who have done them no wrong, in violation of the constitution and the fundamental principles of the government. They no longer acknowledge that all government derives its validity from the consent of the governed. They are about to invade our peaceful homes, destroy our property, and murder our men and dishonor our women. We propose no invasion of the North, no attack on them, and only ask to be left alone."[4]

Later, Cleburne wrote: "It is said slavery is all we are fighting for, and if we give it up we give up all. Even if this were true, which we deny, slavery is not all our enemies are fighting for. It is merely the pretense to establish sectional superiority and a more centralized form of government, and to deprive us of our rights and liberties."[5]

Most of the other Rebels felt the same. Robert Stiles was a Yale graduate and a law student at Columbia University in 1861. He was on the verge of a promising career when the war began but gave it all up to become a private in the Richmond Howitzers, an artillery battalion formed shortly after the John Brown raid. It became part of Robert E. Lee's Army of Northern Virginia. Stiles survived four years of war and became an artillery major. After the war, he wrote: "What now of the essential spirit of these young volunteers? Why did they volunteer? For what did they give their lives?... Surely, it was not for slavery they fought. The great majority of them had never owned a slave, and had little or no interest in that institution. My own father, for example, had freed his slaves long years before... The great conflict will never be properly comprehended by the man who looks upon it as a war for the preservation of slavery."[6]

Dr. Hunter McGuire, Stonewall Jackson's physician and a future president of the American Medical Association, wrote: "The Stonewall Brigade of the Army of Northern Virginia was a fighting organization. I knew every man in it, for I belonged to it for a long time; and I know that I am in proper bounds when I assert, that there was not one soldier in thirty who owned or ever expected to own a slave. The South fighting for the money value of the negro! What a cheap and wicked falsehood!"[7]

When one reads the papers, diaries, and letters of Southern soldiers and civilians alike, these folks were not fighting to protect slavery. Only 6 percent to 7 percent of Confederate enlistees owned slaves. So why did the South fight? Dr. James M. McPherson of Princeton—no friend of the Confederacy—researched thousands of original documents, 25,000 personal letters, and 249 diaries, and produced an answer which will surprise many miseducated high school and college students throughout the country. They were fighting for liberty.[8]

As if to prove their point, Abraham Lincoln moved with incredible speed to suppress freedom and constitutional rights in the North. In the case of Maryland, he had to move quickly. Maryland in those days, while a border state, was Southern in character. Trying to keep it in the Union by constitutional means was too risky, for the loss of Virginia and Maryland meant the loss of Washington, D.C., which was wedged between them. Lincoln therefore faced a choice: act lawlessly or risk losing the capital. Typically, he chose lawlessness.

In April 1861, crowds poured into the streets of Baltimore, the third largest city in the United States. On April 20, the Sixth Massachusetts Infantry Regiment showed up and fired on the rioters, a few of whom also shot at the bluecoats. Four soldiers and at least nine civilians were killed.

The pro-Union governor, Thomas H. Hicks,[9] called the Maryland legislature to meet in Frederick, a town in northwestern Maryland, which was pro-Union, instead of in Annapolis. The legislature rejected a motion to assemble a secession convention but called for the immediate and peaceful recognition of the Confederacy and an end of the U.S. military occupation of Maryland, which they denounced as a "flagrant violation of the Constitution."[10] Governor Hicks declared that Maryland's safety depended on remaining neutral—an impossible plea to anyone who could read a map.

Lincoln responded by suspending the writ of habeas corpus, which was a constitutional safeguard to prevent unlawful imprisonment or imprisonment without due process. Lincoln, Seward, and their henchmen arrested many prominent Marylanders, including thirty-one legislators, the mayor of Baltimore, the chief of police, all of the Baltimore police commissioners, Henry May, a sitting U.S. congressman, the entire Baltimore city council, and dozens of prominent civic leaders, editors, and publishers. Arrests took place in the dead of night so that there would be fewer witnesses. The victims were usually hauled off to Fort Warren, Massachusetts, or some other hellhole where they were incarcerated in crowded casements. If a prisoner asked for a lawyer or tried to send for his family, he was told that this would hurt his case. Often, the victim was jailed based not on what he had done but what he *might* do. Some of them remained in prison until the end of the war.

John Merryman, one of those arrested, appealed to Chief Justice Taney, who was from Maryland. The chief justice wrote a blistering opinion against Lincoln's actions, ruling his executive order was unconstitutional, null, and void. He ordered that a copy of his decision be sent to the Northern president under the seal of the United States Supreme Court. This almost got Taney arrested as well. Lincoln had the arrest warrant drafted but couldn't find any Federal marshals who would execute it.[11]

The fall elections were held shortly thereafter. Federal provost marshals stood guard at the polls, arrested those who were not pro-Union, and granted to U.S. soldiers three-day leaves so they could return home and vote Republican. Voter intimidation kept many pro-Southern Maryland voters far away for the polls. The result was a pro-Union legislature.

With Maryland safely in his pocket, Lincoln acted in total disregard for the Constitution throughout the North. Ohio Congressman Clement Vanlandingham attacked the president's violations of civil liberties, called him "King Lincoln," denounced Wall Street and its war profiteers, as well as the mercantile, manufacturing, and commercial interests, and called for an armistice with the Confederacy. Lincoln's commander of the Department of Ohio—acting under the president's suspension of the writ of habeas corpus—had the congressman arrested, tried by a military court (even though he was a civilian), and thrown into prison for the rest of the war. Lincoln then interceded and expelled him from the country. The president also ordered the arrest of U.S. senator and former vice president John C. Breckinridge of Kentucky. (A handful of Kentucky Confederate soldiers were wounded and captured at Bull Run, and Breckinridge visited them in the hospital, thus proving his "disloyalty.") Breckinridge, however, was warned of his impending arrest and escaped behind Confederate lines before Lincoln's thugs could lay their hands on him.[12] In all, at least 32,000 political prisoners were thrown in jail, and one authority placed the number as high as 40,000.[13] More than 300 newspapers and journals were also shut down. Frequently, the Lincolnites used federal troops to do the dirty work. Printing presses were often smashed and publisher's offices ransacked.

Although they were not having a lot of luck against the Rebels, Lincoln and his minions created a virtual dictatorship over the United States (or what was left of it). William Seward, Lincoln's secretary of state, bragged about his power to Britain's ambassador to the U.S., Lord Lyons. "I can touch a bell on my right hand and order the arrest of a citizen of Ohio. I can touch the bell again and order the arrest of a citizen of New York. Can Queen Victoria do as much?"[14]

"No!" the outraged aristocrat snapped. "Were she to attempt such an act her head would roll from her shoulders."[15]

Meanwhile, Lincoln saw immigrants as key to his political future and success as commander-in-chief. By the time of his 1860 election, one-fourth of the Northern population was immigrants. Dr. Clyde Wilson believed that Lincoln could not have won the election of 1860 without the flood of recent Americans.[16] The Illinois Republican even secretly bought a German-language newspaper to disseminate Republican propaganda to immigrants who were poorly informed about American political issues. After he became president, Lincoln continued to bring in foreigners by the boatload. He also opened Union recruiting offices throughout Europe to hire foreign mercenaries. Some 489,200 mercenaries were recruited from fifteen foreign countries, mostly from Ireland (150,000) and Germany (210,000). Confederate Army officers complained that many of the prisoners they captured could not speak English. Union General Franz Sigel had to have his orders translated from his native German into English and Hungarian. It is doubtful that Lincoln could have won the war without his mercenaries.

If Lincoln favored bringing in Germans and Irish, his attitude toward Negroes was just the opposite. In 1862, he advocated the enactment of a constitutional amendment to buy and deport slaves. He ordered the State Department to approach the European colonial powers to find homes for the African Americans. He explored possibilities in Haiti, Liberia, New Granada, Ecuador, St. Croix, Suriname, British Guiana, Honduras, and the Amazon. Under his compensated emancipation scheme, slavery would end, in phases, by 1900.[17] This led Frederick Douglass to declare in 1876 that, "Mr. Lincoln was pre-eminently the white man's president."[18]

Meanwhile, the war against the South was not going well.

After the war, ex-Confederate soldier Sam Watkins famously declared: "Our cause was lost from the beginning."[19] Watkins deserves our respect, but he was wrong. The South could have won the war in any one of three ways: 1) diplomatically, 2) militarily, or 3) politically.

Diplomatically, many of the upper classes in Great Britain and France would have been delighted to ally with the South against other former colonies. France was additionally motivated by a desire to add Mexico to its empire, despite the Monroe Doctrine. The Lincoln regime gave them an opening on November 8, 1861. That day, Captain Charles Wilkes of the steam frigate USS *San Jacinto* seized the RMS *Trent* and carried off Confederate diplomatic commissioners James Mason and John Slidell. They were taken to the hellish Union prison at Fort Warren, Massachusetts.

When news of the seizure of the *Trent* hit the streets, the North was elated. Captain Wilkes was toasted by Union citizens everywhere. Governor Andrew of Massachusetts held a banquet in his honor, and Congress voted Wilkes a resolution of thanks.

But reality eventually set in.

In London, there was fury. There had been lingering bad blood between America and Britain over rebellion and independence, and the *Trent* incident provoked widespread anger. How dare these colonial upstarts seize a British ship on the high seas and cart off four passengers under the protection of the British flag to a Yankee prison! Secretary of State Seward "is exerting himself to provoke a quarrel with all of Europe," one London newspaper wrote, "in that spirit of senseless egotism which induces the Americans, with their dwarf fleet and shapeless mass of incoherent squads which they call an army, to fancy themselves the equal of France by land and Great Britain by sea."[20]

The USS *San Jacinto* (right) halting RMS *Trent* on the high seas. From Edward S. Ellis, *The Youth's History of the United States* (London: 1887), Vol. 2, 67. *Courtesy of Edward S. Ellis*

The Americans had very clearly misgauged the depth of British outrage. There was serious talk of war. British public opinion was in favor of it by an overwhelming margin. Even some of the most influential anti-slavery voices in the country joined the chorus. Financial markets in New York and London cratered as if war was certain. The value of the U.S. dollar plummeted on the world markets. The British government sent a strongly worded dispatch, demanding an apology and the release of the Confederate commissioners. The U.S. ambassador to London signaled Washington that the British were serious about fighting. The Royal Army sent reinforcements to Canada, more than doubling their ground forces there, and sent 105,000 modern rifles and smoothbores to the province, as well as 20,000,000 cartridges. Two days after the news of the *Trent* arrived, the British cabinet suspended exports of rifles, percussion caps, military stores, and lead to the United States. Worse still, from the Northern point of view, the day he learned of the seizure of the *Trent*, British Foreign Secretary Lord Russell ordered that the export of saltpeter from India to the U.S. be cut off at once. Saltpeter was a necessary ingredient in gunpowder. The U.S. army was effectively paralyzed. With inadequate stockpiles of saltpeter, it was no longer capable of sustaining a major offensive.

Abraham Lincoln, who had cheered the news of the *Trent*, was reluctant to give in to the British threat but, in an emergency cabinet meeting on Christmas morning, 1861, was told he must give in. The United States had to act soon and release the Confederate emissaries or start a war with Britain. Lincoln capitulated on December 26, releasing the Rebel commissioners, who were taken to Provincetown, Massachusetts, and boarded the Royal Navy sloop HMS *Rinaldo*. The British got their apology and a third war with the United Kingdom was averted.

Some of Lincoln's supporters were disappointed by the news; there were still a great many Anglophobes in the United States in 1862. To them, Lincoln would say: "One war at a time, gentlemen. One war at a time."

Despite the successful resolution of the *Trent* affair, it startled Lincoln, who knew the threat of a Franco-Anglo-Confederate alliance was a real one.

He also knew that the British working class was firmly against slavery and that the French would not act without the British. An Emancipation Proclamation freeing Southern slaves could be used, in part, as a diplomatic check against London allying with the South because the British public would not stand for it. Such a proclamation would "drape the invasion of the Southern nation in robes of morality."[21] Born was the Myth of the Noble Cause to free the slaves. The Proclamation might even lead to servile insurrection, Lincoln hoped, forcing the Confederate Army to divert significant resources to the Southern interior to put down slave revolts. The devious Illinois attorney sat down and cleverly drafted the Emancipation Proclamation, which declared slaves free in the secessionist South but nowhere else. Exempted were the Union slave states of Kentucky, Missouri, Maryland, and Delaware, and influential leaders who were slaveholders, including Ulysses S. Grant and William T. Sherman.[22] Some of the parishes in Louisiana were under Union rule. They too were exempt from the Emancipation Proclamation because their confiscated plantations were in the hands of New Englanders, who were in bed with Lincoln politically. William Seward, at least, saw the irony. "We show our sympathy with slavery by emancipating slaves where we cannot reach them, and holding them in bondage where we can set them free," he said.[23] Abolitionist leader Lysander Spooner put it this way: "In short, the North said to the slave-holders: If you will not pay us our price (give us control of your markets) for our assistance against your slaves, we will secure the same price (keep control of your markets) by helping your slaves against you, and using them as our tools for maintaining dominion over you."[24] A popular limerick said it even better. "Lincoln, Lincoln, wily wretch, freed the slaves he couldn't catch."

Lincoln knew his Emancipation Proclamation was unconstitutional, but he justified it as a temporary war measure. Of course, he knew that he could always renege on it later, if needed. In his State of the Union Address of December 1862, Lincoln offered the Southern states an opportunity to retain their slaves until January 1, 1900, along with financial compensation to any slave owners and a promise to remove all blacks to Africa or Latin America.[25]

Unfortunately for Lincoln, Southern black people were not so stupid. There were no slave revolts. Why should they revolt? If the Union Army arrived in their area, they would be freed, or so they thought. If they revolted before that, they would quite likely face fully armed and angry Rebels in disciplined formations, led by skilled and veteran combat officers, while they had only knives, rocks, and pitchforks. And every one of them knew the penalty for servile insurrection was death, a penalty the Rebels could be counted on to extract. Better to wait for the Yankee army.

"Honest Abe" did not gain everything he wanted from the Emancipation Proclamation, but he got most of it. The Confederacy had lost the chance to win the war diplomatically. Only the military and political options remained after January 1, 1863.[26]

• • •

Meanwhile, Abraham Lincoln was again having trouble with his own people.

As incredible as this statement may sound to certain modern readers, New York City was sympathetic to the South as the Civil War approached. It voted against Lincoln by a two to one margin in 1860, and its mayor, Democrat Fernando Wood, threatened to secede from both Albany and Washington in 1861. By 1863, the total population of the city was 813,669. Half of the population consisted of immigrants, and most of these were Irish, who lived in incredible poverty. The new arrivals were poor and not favorably disposed towards African American men, with whom they were competing for low-wage jobs. Corporate employers naturally took advantage of this situation to keep wages low for immigrants and blacks alike. In general, Irish and blacks were destitute, due to low wages.

In March 1863, white New York City longshoremen or dock workers were on strike for higher pay. The corporate bosses brought in black strikebreakers to take their jobs. One day, strikers attacked 200 of these African Americans. Armed guards had to protect them. There were no fatalities reported, although there were injuries on both sides.

Labor unrest continued in New York City throughout the Civil War.

Meanwhile, throughout the North, the allure and romance of the war evaporated under the withering fire of Confederate rifles and muskets. Voluntary Union enlistments slowed to a trickle. Due to his many military defeats and heavy casualties, Lincoln instituted a draft to fill his depleted ranks. Rich people, those who could pay $300 ($6,069.07 in 2017 money[27]), were exempt from conscription. Excused from the draft were African Americans, who were not considered citizens yet. The striking longshoremen were already angry over wages. Now they faced being drafted into the Union Army to, as James Howell Street wrote, "face death to give freedom to Negro slaves whose cousins had taken their jobs."

"It was too much."[28]

The first drawing for the draft in New York City occurred on July 11, 1863. On July 13, a crowd of 500 people turned itself into a mob. Led by longshoremen and firefighters, it began the most lethal riot in American history. It lasted four days. Several regiments of Union troops had to be recalled from Pennsylvania; soldiers and police fired into the mob with cannons, muskets, and rifles; and police busted skulls with heavy locust wood clubs, tossed rock throwers off the roofs of buildings, and shot them with revolvers. One authority estimated that more than 2,000 people died and some 8,000 had been injured.[29] Many African Americans were lynched, drowned, tortured, or set on fire.

New York City draft rioters exchanging gunfire with Union Army troops, July 1863. *Courtesy of the Illustrated London News*

In reality, the rioters won the conflict, despite the casualties. New York City agreed to pay the $300 exemption fee for those who could not afford it. The mob got what they wanted. They would not have to risk death for "the Glorious Union." Since many African Americans fled the city, black labor competition was reduced.

Anti-draft riots took place in other Northern cities in July 1863, including Detroit; Buffalo and Troy, New York; Cincinnati; Boston; Portsmouth, New Hampshire; Rutland, Vermont; and Wooster, Ohio.[30] They were not as bad as those in New York City, which were the worst in U.S. history. Taken as a whole, the New York Draft Riots witnessed one of the largest mass lynching of innocent blacks in American history.

* * *

Lynching and hanging are, of course, different things. Hangings are legal. The Lincoln administration set the record for the largest mass hanging in American history conducted against a minority group in 1862. Following the suppression of an Indian uprising, a military tribunal found 303 Dakota (eastern Sioux) guilty of rape and murder. (Military tribunals are usually organized to convict.) Abraham Lincoln thought this was too many to kill all at once, so he granted clemency to all but thirty-eight; they were hanged at Mankoto, Minnesota, on December 28, 1862.

* * *

The South lost its chances to win the war militarily at the Battle of Gettysburg and when Vicksburg fell. It still could have won the war by political means if the North had agreed to a negotiated peace. This could only occur if Lincoln were defeated in the upcoming election, which was possible in the summer of 1864. Even Lincoln worried he was going to lose. But the Southern leadership mishandled the military situation on the western front in 1864. After Atlanta fell on September 2, Northern public opinion completely reversed itself, thinking the end of the war was in sight. Lincoln was handily reelected on November 8, and the political solution was no longer a realistic choice. The South was out of options.

Meanwhile, the wealth redistribution from South to North took a more direct form.

Some Union generals, such as Don Carlos Buell and Benjamin Grierson, kept their men in check. They insisted that their soldiers follow the rules of civilized warfare and were strong enough to compel even their white trash troops to obey orders. Not every bluecoat commander had such strength or sterling moral character, and some of them opposed nineteenth-century "civilized warfare." There was a cultural saying then: "There are some things a gentleman will not do." Waging war against defenseless women and children was one of those things. Abraham Lincoln, however, did not feel so constrained. He encouraged and supported a barbaric form of conflict, which his willing accomplices called "total war." It began in April 1862, when Colonel Ival Vasilovitch Turchinoff, a former Russian officer, entered Athens, Alabama, with the Nineteenth and Twenty-fourth Illinois Infantry Regiments. Now going by the alias John B. Turchin, Turchinoff encouraged his men to commit many atrocities against the defenseless civilians of the town. Drunk federals robbed stores, broke into private homes, burned, pillaged and raped. Several women—both black and white—were assaulted sexually at bayonet point, and one pregnant woman miscarried after she was gang raped. This went on for some time. When Turchinoff's commanding officer, General Buell, learned what had happened, he had the Russian court-martialed. Found guilty, Turchinoff was dishonorably discharged on August 6, 1862. Lincoln not only set aside the verdict; he promoted the disgraced officer to brigadier general.[31]

Athens set the stage for later outrageous behavior and an even more direct form of wealth transfer than the tariff. In May 1863, for example, U.S. major general James B. McPherson headquartered at "Ashwood" plantation, the home of Mrs. Elizabeth Meade Ingraham. McPherson refused to protect the place, and his men looted it for days. The general personally took part in the pillaging. He and his staff stole two five-gallon demijohns of whiskey.[32] The men broke into Mrs. Ingraham's home, opened the dining room closet with a hatchet, and took the family's silver and table linen. They stole or broke every pan, pitcher, cup, plate, etc., and stole buggies, wagons, and every horse and mule—except one who was about to foal and refused to move. They shot all the sheep, killed or stole all the cattle, and shot all but four of the hogs. They even made off with dresses, sheets, and blankets. They destroyed all of the portraits of deceased family members and even stole her Bibles, although "What such rascals want with Bibles I can't tell," Mrs. Ingraham noted caustically in her diary.[33] Ironically, Mrs. Ingraham was not from Mississippi. She was from Philadelphia, Pennsylvania, but she suffered a fate similar to many Southern women.

As Ashwood was being ravished, Mrs. Ingraham interviewed the plunderers and asked them if they were fighting to free the slaves. Every one of them denied it. As if to prove their point, the bluecoats went to the slave quarters, where they robbed the African Americans at gunpoint and sacked their homes. Kate, a former slave who had been victimized, walked up to Union Brigadier General Charles E. Hovey and told him to his face that the Yankees "came to rob the negroes, not to protect them."[34]

That very day, in Virginia, Mrs. Ingraham's brother, Major General George G. Meade, was commanding the U.S. V Corps against Robert E. Lee in the Battle of Chancellorsville. Two months later, he would command the Army of the Potomac at Gettysburg, which (along with Vicksburg) would be one of the decisive battles of the war.

●●●

Mrs. Ingraham's experience was not unusual. Throughout the Confederacy, the Union conquest was marked by wanton pillaging, malicious cruelty, and rape. In Oxford, Mississippi, Jacob Thompson's beautiful mansion, "Home Place," held $100,000 worth of furnishings (about $2,200,000 in 2018 dollars). Union general Hatch personally pillaged it, stealing silver plates, china, furniture, silverware, and other items of value. He carried it off in an ambulance. General A. J. "Whiskey" Smith, who was as cruel as Sherman, personally sent one of his staff officers and a detachment of men to destroy "Home Place."

Oxford, Mississippi, circa 1865. *Courtesy of Jack Case Wilson, "Faulkners, Fortunes and Flames"*

Given only fifteen minutes, Mrs. Catherine Ann Thompson removed her few remaining valuables before it was burned.[35] As she was leaving, a squad of blue-coated liberators robbed her at gunpoint. She was left with nothing. Other defenseless citizens, black and white, were whipped or sexually molested. "The public square was surrounded by a canopy of flames," one Federal recorded, " ... In fact, where once stood a handsome little country town, now only remained the blackened skeletons of houses, and the smoldering ruins that marked the track of war."[36]

This was widespread throughout most of the South.

"We have had a glorious time in this State," U.S. army lieutenant Thomas J. Myers wrote to his wife in Boston from South Carolina in early 1865.

Unrestricted license to burn and plunder was the order of the day. The civility have been stripped of most of their valuables. Gold watches, silver, pitchers, cups, spoons, forks, and so forth are as common in camp as blackberries...

Officers are not allowed to join in these expeditions unless disguised as privates. One of our corps commanders borrowed a rough suit of clothes from one of my men and was successful in his place. He got a large quantity of silver among other things… and a very fine watch from a Mr. DeSaussure of this place.

… I have a quart—I am not joking—I have at least a quart of jewelry for you and the girls and some No. 1 diamond pins and rings among them. General Sherman has gold and silver enough to start a bank.

Myers added: "The damned niggers, as a general thing, preferred to stay at home particularly after they found that we wanted only the able bodied men and to tell the truth the youngest and best looking women.… "[37]

Columbia, South Carolina, 1865, after Sherman burned it. *Courtesy of George C. Barnard, National Archives*

The end came at Appomattox Court House on April 9, 1865, when Robert E. Lee surrendered to General Grant. The last Rebel forces surrendered by June, and the surviving veterans returned to a devastated landscape. And so the South returned to the United States. Abraham Lincoln saved the Union in much the same way an abusive husband saves a marriage when his long-suffering wife—tired after years of mistreatment and exploitation—announces her intention to leave. He grabs her by the throat and beats her until she submits. Here the analogy breaks down, however. An abused wife might be able to turn to charities, police authorities, her church, or family for help. The South was on its own. Rather than help, the government was more interested in stealing what remained after the destruction.

CHAPTER XV

THE COSTS AND RESULTS OF THE WAR

Sirs, you have no reason to be ashamed of your Confederate dead; see to it they have no reason to be ashamed of you.

—*Colonel Rev. Robert Lewis Dabney, D.D. chief of staff to Stonewall Jackson*

... the consolidation of the states into one vast empire, sure to be aggressive abroad and despotic at home, will be the certain precursor of ruin which has overwhelmed all that preceeded it.

—*Robert E. Lee*[1]

Dr. Livingston wrote that, if the recent estimate of 750,000 killed in the war is accepted, the total number of deaths as a result of the Civil War was about 1,000,000.[2] Thousands of Southerners died in the aftermath of the war from starvation, malnutrition, disease, or injury. African-Americans, at the bottom of the economic pile, suffered a disproportionately high number of fatalities. Figures are difficult to obtain, however. The Union Army occupied the South at that time, and its scorched-earth policies caused starvation. Certainly, the Union Army had little interest in the unfolding tragedy around it, or soldiers wouldhave prevented so many black deaths.

In fact, one cost ignored by establishment historians for far too long was the cost in terms of death and destruction caused to black people by Mr. Lincoln's War and Emancipation Proclamation. One ridiculous, self-righteous historian went so far as to proclaim that the war resulted in "620,000 dead, 4,000,000 freed." Had this person analyzed the results of the conflict better, he might not have made such a silly statement. Historian Jim Downs broached the subject of the cost of emancipation with his masterpiece, *Sick From Freedom: African American Death and Suffering During the Civil War and Reconstruction*, which should have won a Pulitzer Prize. "The Civil War," he writes, "produced the largest biological crisis of the nineteenth century... wreaking havoc on the population of the newly freed." Tens of thousands of freed slaves died due to the "exigencies of war and the massive dislocation triggered by emancipation."[3] Downs estimated that 1,000,000 of the 4,000,000 freed slaves suffered serious illness or death. We do not know how many died, but there were tens of thousands of deaths, especially among black children.[4]

Other costs are easier to estimate. The South lost about 60 percent of its capital; one in four of its young men of military age killed; one in four others crippled; its currency worthless; and its society and economy systematically destroyed. The true value of Southern property fell from $6.3 billion to $4.2 billion. At the same time, the true value of United States' property increased from $16.2 billion to $30.1 billion. The South's share of the value of property in the United States (excluding slaves) fell from 39 percent in 1860 to less than 15 percent ($4.2 billion). According to Dr. Johnson, the property valuation of the South in 1870 was only 59 percent of what it had been in 1860. If the loss in value of the freed slaves is included in the calculation, this figure drops to 37 percent.[5] During the same period, Northern property values almost doubled.

● ● ●

Southern slavery and its aftermath were not solely Southern wrongs. It was, as Dr. Livingston pointed out, the country's duty to emancipate the slaves, to compensate the slave owners for their losses, and to integrate freed blacks into American society.[6] Nothing like this happened.

During the antebellum period, not a single political party advocated emancipation. And none advanced the ideas of compensation and integration beyond words.

Until the 1960s, historians did not believe the war was only about slavery, despite the Myth of the Noble Cause. For most, it was all about restoring the Union and coast-to-coast economic nationalism, controlled by Northern financial and commercial interests.[7] The idea that it was all about the moral issue of slavery is a relatively recent view—in spite of an enormous amount of historical evidence to the contrary.

Had there been no war, evidence suggests that an independent Confederacy would have ended slavery like other countries in the Western Hemisphere, and race relations in the South (and in America) would be better than they are now. While impossible to predict history with any certainty, an important indicator is that there were more free black people in the South than in the North in 1860.[8] Every other country in the world except Haiti freed its slaves without war. Is there any reason to believe it could not have happened here? No, given the history throughout the Western Hemisphere, it was more likely to happen than not. The agitation of the abolitionists and the greed of the Northern financial, mercantile, industrial, railroad, and commercial interests were the real roadblocks to freedom. This explosive agitation culminated in the election of the unscrupulous Lincoln and the passage of the punitive Morrill Tariff, which was not replaced until 1913.

Given what we know in other countries nearby, the Civil War probably ended slavery only thirty to thirty-five years earlier than would have been the case had the institution been allowed to die out organically. The South (including blacks) would have been spared a brutal war, the scorched-earth policy of certain Union war criminals, plunder, pillaging, starvation, military dictatorship, a decade of military occupation, the incredible corruption of Reconstruction, the manipulation of black people by the Republican party to keep itself in power, and the needless deaths of tens of thousands (and probably hundreds of thousands) of freed black people. Millions of people (both white and African-American) would have been spared the crushing poverty of the New South era.

With typical foresight, the Lincoln regime issued the Emancipation Proclamation to encourage slave revolts and end the possibility of a diplomatic alliance between the Confederacy, Britain, and France. It sought to use people of color for its own purposes but made no provisions for the suddenly displaced African Americans, and indeed, there is no evidence they even thought about them. The Yankee generals dubbed them "contrabands," a derogatory term never used by the Rebels and roughly equal to the word *Untermenschen* (subhumans), a term the Germans used in the 1930s and 1940s to describe Jews, Slavs, and other people they considered inferior. They tossed them into "contraband camps," which were the first modern concentration camps. They were no longer slaves, but they were not full American citizens either and had almost nothing in the way of civil rights. Able-bodied men were separated from their families and forced to work on plantations, which were under Northern management. They faced being defrauded of their minimum wages or not paid at all. In some camps, there were also multiple rapes of black women by Union soldiers every night.[9]

As early as 1863, the Union Army was leasing plantations to people later called "Carpetbaggers." The freemen on the plantations were supposed to be paid $7 per month. Women received $5 per month, and children received half as much pay as adults. They were often not paid, however. The new lessees, Private Samuel H. Glasgow of the Twenty-Third Iowa wrote, "did not have the best interests of the former slave at heart… Cotton closes their eyes to justice, just as it did in the case of the former slave masters," he wrote.[10] Many black people didn't find their situations on the leased plantations much better than slavery. Often treated brutally, they were unable to leave. U.S. brigadier general John P. Hawkins, the chief commissary of the XIII Corps and a "true believer" abolitionist, castigated the new lessees, stating that the new plantation system was "nothing but a system of slavery" and even suggested that, if better employers could not be found than these people, the army should "send for their former masters and tell each one to claim his slaves, [because] his treatment of them was parental compared to what we now permit."[11] This was an astonishing recommendation, given its source.[12]

Overcrowded contraband camps were unsanitary and usually devoid of even the most primitive medical facilities. The Union Army had none of the training, the resources, or the will to deal with the situation. Malnutrition was common. Tens of thousands died. The U.S. Army contributed to the mortality rate by force-marching some of the camps to new locations, some hundreds of miles away.

The suffering of the African Americans continued after the South surrendered. Many acres of Southern land lay uncultivated and in ruin during and after the conflict. The years 1866 and 1867 brought low yields and crop failures, and 1867 was a year of famine, with mortality rates which Downs described as "chilling."[13]

Smallpox epidemics periodically raged throughout the South and West from 1862 through 1868. Weakened and malnourished black people were especially susceptible, often dying at rates three or four times higher than Southern whites, who were themselves malnourished. Black children were particularly hard hit. In one six-month period in 1865, 30,000 died in North Carolina and South Carolina alone. The epidemic lasted six years.[14]

Things were only a little better for white Southerners. Tax rates in the South were 300 percent to 400 percent higher than they had been in 1860, even though property values had declined significantly. People simply could not pay their taxes. In 1871, 3,300,000 acres were for sale in Mississippi due to tax defaults. This amounted to 15 percent of all taxable land.[15] The corrupt Republican carpetbaggers and Southern collaborators (called scalawags) got nearly all of it. Almost none of the revenue so generated went to the black population or ex-Confederates.

● ● ●

Incidentally, after the war, Southern attitudes toward slavery changed—or they just admitted what they thought all along. Slavery, most of them proclaimed, was wrong, although they steadfastly denied that it was cruel. The survivors of the antebellum South went to their graves firm in this opinion.

•••

The years of President Grant's administration have gone down as the most corrupt in American history.[16] It did not begin there, however. It had a long run-up, starting with the first protective tariff of 1816, when Northern special interest groups realized they could get rich feasting at the public trough. But the corruption of the 1820s was nothing compared to that of the late 1860s and 1870s, when it was incredibly widespread. The South Carolina legislature, for example, appropriated $1,000 to cover the gambling losses of the speaker of the house on a horse race. Carpetbagger Governor William P. Kellogg of Louisiana said: "I don't pretend to be honest… Corruption is the fashion."[17] Carpetbagger Governor Adelbert Ames of Mississippi (a former Union general from Maine), reportedly paid a prostitute $100,000 in state bonds for her services. This kind of overt corruption continued for six years and, in some cases, ten.

Reconstruction was, to paraphrase Karl von Clausewitz, conducting war by other means. The Carpetbaggers plundered the South as badly as did Sherman's "bummers"—and perhaps they were worse. The South has yet to regain its position of prosperity vis-à-vis the North.[18] Not one Southern state after the war was in the top ten in per capita income. In 1860, five were.

Eventually, the Carpetbaggers fled back to the north with their ill-gotten gains. Southern blacks—who had served their political purposes—were abandoned to Southern whites, whom the departed Northern political thugs had so long denounced as heartless brutes. Home rule was re-established in the South, but it took Dixie decades to recover economically. Reconstruction left behind a system of segregation and peonage (sharecropping) that did not exist before the war (a separate story, beyond the scope of this book).[19]

It should be clear by now to any open-minded reader that the war was not just about slavery and certainly not primarily about slavery. It was chiefly about money. The main result of the war was settling the issue of "What kind of government would we have?" From 1783 to 1865, there was a struggle between the Hamiltonian ideas of a strong, central government (with the corruption which naturally accompanied it) and the small government ideas of Jefferson, with a system of checks and balances, and the sense of personal responsibility that naturally accompanies it. The Hamiltonian system called for principal loyalty to a strong, dominant federal government. The Jeffersonian ideal held that the principal loyalty was to be to the state and to the idea that that "governs best which governs least." The issue is now settled. Hamiltonianism eventually (and naturally) evolved into the present Nanny State. People look to an ever-growing government for most everything. In a recent instance, someone called 911 because McDonald's had not included any catsup for his French fries in his to-go order. This is a good example of how far certain people have allowed dependency on the government to seep into their minds. The catsup incident is an extreme case, to be sure, but it is not *that* extreme. Since 1865, the only restraint to the federal government *has been* the federal government—an oxymoron that works for very few Americans today.

NOTES

Introduction

1. Grady McWhiney, "Jefferson Davis, the Unforgiven," *Journal of Mississippi History*, Vol. XLII (May 1980), 124. Dr. Grady McWhiney (1928–2006) was a native of Shreveport, Louisiana. He graduated from Columbia and became a great scholar. He taught in several institutions, including the University of California at Berkeley, the University of Alabama, Texas Christian University, and the University of Southern Mississippi.
2. Raphael Semmes, *Memoirs of Service Afloat* (Baltimore: 1869), v.
3. "Contributed Quotes," Quotations Page, http://www.quotationspage.com/quote/37218.html.
4. J. W. Schuckers, *The Life and Public Service of Salmon Portland Chase* (New York: 1874), 533.
5. See Shelby Foote, *The Civil War: A Narrative*, Volume 3, *Red River to Appomattox* (New York: 1986), 1035.

Chapter I: Slavery and the Yankee Flesh Peddler

1. R. Michael Givens, "Introduction," in *To Live and Die in Dixie*, ed. Frank B. Powell, III (Columbia, Tennessee: 2014), vii. R. Michael Givens was the commander in chief of the Sons of Confederate Veterans from 2010 to 2014.
2. Adam Taylor, "There Are an Estimated 40 Million Slaves in the World. Where Do They Live and What Do They Do?" *Washington Post*, September 19, 2017, https://www.washingtonpost.com/news/worldviews/wp/2017/09/19/there-are-an-estimated-40-million-slaves-in-the-world-where-do-they-live-

andwhat- do-they-do/?utm_term=.1ea81bdf0c46. If the reader is interested in further information on modern slavery, the Walk Free Foundation publishes an annual report called the Global Slavery Index.

3.   James Ronald Kennedy and Walter Donald Kennedy, *The South Was Right!* (Gretna, Louisiana: 2004), 2nd ed., 63.

4.   R. W. Fogel and S. L. Engerman, *Time on the Cross* (Boston: 1974), 17.

5.   Donald Livingston, "Why the War Was Not about Slavery," in *To Live and Die in Dixie,* ed. Frank B. Powell, III (Columbia, Tennessee: 2014), 2.

6.   Theodore Canot, *Captain Canot or Twenty Years of an African Slaver* (New York: 1854), 62.

7.   Ibid., 90.

8.   Ibid., 91-95.

9.   Ibid., 101. See Richard Drake, *Revelations of a Slave Smuggler* (New York: 1860), for the story of a Bostonian who was a slaver for fifty years. Also see George Francis Dow, *Slave Ships and Slaving* (Cambridge, Maryland: 1968).

10.   "Inflation Calculator," In2013dollars.com, http://www.in2013dollars. com/1827-dollars-in-2016?amount=41438. These are the latest available figures.

11.   Daniel P. Mannix, *Black Cargoes* (New York: 1962), 245.

12.   Ibid., 166.

13.   Adele Oltman, "The Hidden History of Slavery in New York," *The Nation,* November 7, 2005.

14.   Henry Louis Gates, Jr., "Ending the Slavery Blame-Game," *New York Times,* April 23, 2010, A27. Dr. Gates was the Alphonse Fletcher University Professor and Director of the Hutchins Center for African and African American Research at Harvard University in 2010.

15.   Ibid.

16.   Sir Richard Burton, *A Mission to Gelele, King of Dahome* (London: 1864), http://burtoniana.org/books/1864-A%20Mission%20to%20Gelele%20 King%20of%20Dahome/A_Mission_to_Gelele__King_of_Dahome%20 vol%20I.pdf.

17.   Gates, "Ending the Slavery Blame-Game," A27.

18.   Lorenzo Johnston Greene, *The Negro in Colonial New England, 1620–1776* (New York: 1942), 138; Edgar J. McManus, *Black Bondage in the North* (Syracuse: 1970), 169–70, http://www.slavenorth.com.

19.   Ibid.

20.   Livingston, 2, citing Joanne Pope Melish, *Disowning Slavery, Gradual Emancipation and Race in New England, 1780–1860* (Ithaca, New York: 1998), xii–xiv, 7, 17.

21.   Clyde Wilson, "Those People," in *To Live and Die in Dixie,* ed. Frank B. Powell, III (Columbia, Tennessee: 2014), 47.

22.   Temple Franklin Cooper was born in South Carolina on July 19, 1805, and died on February 2, 1864, on Johnson Island, Ohio, and is buried there in Erie Cemetery. His great-grandfather was William Franklin, the Royal Governor of New Jersey. He commanded Company K, Fifty-Second Georgia Infantry Regiment, and was captured in the Battle of Champion Hill, May 1863.

23. George H. Moore, *Notes on the History of Slavery in Massachusetts* (New York: 1866), 30, 88.

24. Estimates of the number of slaves taken from Africa vary considerably. I have seen estimates as low as 12,500,000. The sad truth is we do not know with any degree of certainty how many Africans were taken from their homeland.

Chapter II: Hypocrisy

1. "Statistics on Slavery," Weber Unniversity, faculty.weber.edu/kmackay/statistics_on_slavery.htm.

2. "Witchhunt in New York: The 1741 Rebellion," https://pbs.org/wgbh/aia/part1/1p286.html; Daniel Horsmanden, "The New York Conspiracy of 1741," in the Gilder Institute of American History, https://gilderlehrman.org/content/new-york-conspiracy-1741; E. W. R. Ewing, *Northern Rebellion and Southern Secession* (Richmond, Virginia: 1904), 77.

3. See Jeffrey R. Hummel, *Emancipating Slaves, Enslaving Free Men* (Chicago: 1996).

4. Ibid., 10.

5. Manumission takes place when owners free their slaves voluntarily. Emancipation is the process of freeing slaves through government action. Emancipation is done gradually and can involve compensation. Abolition is when a government ends slavery completely. It can be done all at once or in increments. No compensation is required.

6. McManus, *Black Bondage in the North*, 168.

7. Ibid., 182.

8. Solomon Northup, Sue Eakin, and Joseph Logsdon, eds., *Twelve Years a Slave* (1853; reprint ed., Baton Rouge: 1996), 62.

9. See Northup, Eakin, and Logsdon, eds., *Twelve Years a Slave* from which most of this passage is drawn.

10. McManus, *Black Bondage in the North*, 180.

11. Beverly B. Munford, *Virginia's Attitude Toward Slavery and Secession*. (Richmond: 2nd School Ed., 1914), 171.

12. Livingston, "Why the War Was Not about Slavery,"13.

13. Hummel, *Emancipating Slaves, Enslaving Free Men*, 10.

14. Contrary to myth, Eli Whitney did not invent the cotton gin. People had been ginning black seed cotton in India and Africa since before recorded history. Whitney invented a machine which would gin green seed cotton, which was grown in North America. Whitney later remarked that sometimes an invention can be so important as to be useless to the inventor. His patent (which was dated March 14, 1794) was soon infringed upon. He sued twice and lost twice. He made his fortune by originating the interchangeable parts of firearms. He also invented the desk in which all drawers could be locked by locking only the central drawer instead of having to lock all drawers individually. (He had grandchildren who liked to pilfer.)

15. The Petit Gulf variety of cotton combined high yields with a relatively short growing season.

16. Hummel, *Emancipating Slaves, Enslaving Free Men*, 44. In many cases, the Mexican slaves purchased their own freedom and that of their families.
17. Brazil ended slavery in 1888.
18. Livingston, "Why the War Was Not about Slavery," 9; Anne Farrow, Joel Lang, and Jennifer Frank, *How the North Promoted, Prolonged and Profited from Slavery* (New York: 2005), 110.
19. George Francis Dow, *Slave Ships and Slaving* (Cambridge, Maryland: 1927), 21.
20. H. V. Traywick Jr., "Unlearning 'Fake History,'" The Abbeville Blog, The Abbeville Institute: April 25, 2018.
21. Ibid.
22. Ibid.
23. W. E. Burghardt Du Bois, *The Suppression of the African Slave-Trade to the United States of America, 1638–1870* (1896; reprint ed., New York: 1904), 179.
24. Traywick, "Unlearning 'Fake History.'"

Chapter III: Secession

1. Lysander Spooner, *No Treason: The Constitution of No Authority* (1870; reprint ed., Free Patriot Press: n.d.), 1.
2. Shelby Foote (1916–2005), Interview posted on YouTube, 2016.
3. "From Thomas Jefferson to Abigail Smith Adams, 11 September 1804," Jefferson Papers, National Archives, https://founders.archives.gov/documents/Jefferson/99-01-02-0348.
4. Donald W. Livingston, "Confederate Emancipation Without War," in *To Live and Die in Dixie,* ed. Frank B. Powell, III (Columbia, Tennessee: 2014), 456. Dr. Livingston is a professor of philosophy at Emory University and is the former president of the prestigious and highly acclaimed Abbeville Institute.
5. Ibid.
6. Charles Francis Adams, *Lee at Appomattox, And Other Papers* (Boston and New York: 1902), 387. Charles Francis was the grandson of President John Quincy Adams.
7. Shelby Foote, interview posted on YouTube, 2016.
8. South Carolina considered seceding during the Nullification Crisis of 1832–1833 (see Chapter 5).

Chapter IV: Pregnant Events

1. As a rule, tariffs of 20 percent or above were considered protective. Anything below about 15 percent was looked upon as a revenue tariff. The 15 to 20 percent tariff could be classified as protective or revenue, depending on who was doing the classifying.
2. Andrew P. Napolitano, *The Constitution in Exile* (Nashville, Tennessee: 2006), 238.
3. Karen Stokes, "The Morrill Tariff," in *To Live and Die in Dixie,* ed. Frank B. Powell, III (Columbia, Tennessee: 2014), 144.
4. Livingston, 6.

5. During the US Constitutional Convention of 1787, some states wanted a slave to be counted as a full person for electoral purposes. Others did not think they should be counted at all. The result was a compromise: slaves were counted as three-fifths of a person for purposes of the Electoral College and apportioning the US House of Representatives.
6. Livingston, 7, citing Farrow et al., 183.
7. Livingston, 7.
8. John Randolph of Roanoke (1773-1833) was known for his passion (especially for education for all), his oratory, and his quick wit. At various times, he was a congressman, a senator, and US ambassador to Russia. An ally of Jefferson, he believed states had the right to judge the constitutionality of measures passed by the national government and nullify them if need be.
9. Thomas DiLorenzo, *The Real Lincoln* (New York: 2002; New York: 2003), 27.
10. Although undoubtedly important, the issue of a national bank will not be addressed in any great detail in this book, because it was more a political, rather than a sectional, issue. It should be noted, however, that the bank would have been controlled by Northern, not Southern or Western, interests.
11. Norris W. Preyer, "Southern Support of the Tariff of 1816: A Reappraisal," *Journal of Southern History*, Vol. XXV (August 1959), in *Essays on Jacksonian America, ed.* Frank O. Gatell (New York: 1970), 20.
12. Tallmadge (1778-1853) only served a single term in Congress, but he was later lieutenant governor of New York. He was also instrumental in the founding of New York University.
13. Livingston, 12.
14. Ibid., 8.
15. Clay introduced the "American System" in 1817. Hamilton was shot in a duel on July 11, 1804, and died the next day.
16. Constitution of the United States, Article I, Section 8, Clause 1, and other clauses.
17. Leonard M. Scruggs, "The Morrill Tariff," in *To Live and Die in Dixie*, ed. Frank B. Powell, III (Columbia, Tennessee: 2014), 147.
18. James Spence, *The American Union* (London: 1862), 180.
19. Linda Barnickel, *Milliken's Bend: A Civil War Battle in History and Memory* (Baton Rouge, Louisiana: 2013), 13.

Chapter V: The Nullification Crisis
1. The Suffolk Resolves was a declaration by the leaders of Suffolk County, Massachusetts, rejecting the Massachusetts Government Act and resolving to boycott goods imported from Britain until repeal of the Intolerable Acts.
2. Tennessee became the sixteenth state on June 16, 1796. It apparently saw no need to ratify the amendment, since three-quarters of the states had already approved it, and it had, in effect, already been ratified.
3. Thomas A. Bailey and David M. Kennedy, *The American Pageant* (Lexington, Massachusetts, and Toronto, Canada, 7th ed.: 1983), Vol. I, 169.
4. There were only thirty-five district courts at this time. Now there are 673 district judges and 179 appellate judges.

5. Livingston, "Confederate Emancipation," 468.
6. Clifford Dowdey, *Lee* (New York: 1965), 58; Livingston, "Confederate Emancipation," 468.
7. Dowdey, *Lee*, 58.
8. Livingston, "Confederate Emancipation," 468.
9. Dean Wilson, North Carolina State University lecture, 1973.
10. The AME Church in Charleston had almost 2,000 members in 1822. It was the second largest AME Church in the United States at that time, behind the one in Philadelphia.
11. Wilson, "Those People II" citing Thomas Jefferson's letter to John Holmes, April 22, 1820, and to William Branch Giles, December 26, 1825.
12. David J. Eicher, *The Longest Night: A Military History of the Civil War* (New York: 2002), 41.
13. H. A. Scott Trask, "Who Won the Webster-Hayne Debate of 1830?" *The Abbeville Review*, Abbeville Institute, August 30, 2016, 1–16.
14. Ibid., 4.
15. Ibid., 6.
16. McDuffie (1790–1851) was born in Georgia and was well-educated at the Willington Academy, one of the most famous private academies of its day. A successful attorney, he initially opposed states' rights but converted to nullification by 1828. Seriously wounded in a duel in 1822, his personality changed, and he became highly irritable most of the time. He served in the South Carolina Assembly from 1818 to 1821 and a congressman from 1821 to 1834. He was the fifty-fifth governor of South Carolina (1834–36) and a U.S. senator (1842–46).
17. Scruggs, "The Morrill Tariff," 151, citing John Niven, *John C. Calhoun and the Price of Union* (Baton Rouge: 1988), 172–73.
18. James Hamilton, Jr. (1786–1857) was the mayor of Charleston who put down the Denmark Vesey Revolt in 1822. He served in the US House of Representatives (1822–1829) before becoming governor on December 9, 1830. His term expired on December 10, 1832. After he left office, Hayne appointed him brigadier general of state militia. Poor business decisions left him financially destitute in the 1830s, and he held no further public offices. He moved to Texas in 1855. Hamilton died a hero. He was aboard a steamboat which sank in the Gulf of Mexico. Hamilton drowned after giving up his seat on a lifeboat to save a mother and her child.
19. Robert Young Hayne (1791–1839) was born into a planter family in the Colleton District of South Carolina. He studied law, gained admission to the bar, and practiced in Charleston. He was a captain in the 3rd South Carolina Infantry Regiment during the War of 1812 and was later quartermaster general of the State Militia. He was a member of the state House of Representatives (1814–18) and briefly served as speaker (1818) before becoming state attorney general (1818–22). His former colleagues in the legislature elected him U.S. senator in 1822, and he served until 1832. Hayne was governor from December 13, 1832, to December 11, 1834. His last public service was as mayor of Charleston (1836–37).

Chapter VI: Cultural Differences

1. Kennedy and Kennedy, *The South Was Right!*, 23, citing Trollope, as quoted in Sir James Marshall-Cornwall, *Grant as a Military Commander* (New York: 1970), 5.

2. Kennedy and Kennedy, *The South Was Right!*, 24, citing Anthony Trollope, *North America* (New York: 1951), 351.

3. Kennedy and Kennedy, *The South Was Right!*, 24, citing Lagniappe, *A Journal of the Old South* (Spring, 1974), 32.

4. David H. Fischer, *Albion's Seed* (Oxford: 1989), 6.

5. Wilson, "Those People," 46–47.

6. Ibid., 50.

7. Alexis de Tocqueville, *Democracy in America*, ed. J. P. Mayer (1835; reprint ed., New York: 1969), 343.

8. Livingston, "Confederate Emancipation," 468, citing *Lincoln Speeches and Writings, ed.* Don E. Fehrenbacher (New York: 1989), 478.

9. Hummel, *Emancipating Slaves, Enslaving Free Men,* 57.

10. James Ronald Kennedy and Walter Donald Kennedy, *Punished with Poverty*, (Columbia, South Carolina: 2016), 27–28.

11. Unfortunately, when I last accessed this site (2016), one state's narratives were missing: those from Louisiana.

12. See C. Vann Woodward, *The Strange Career of Jim Crow* (New York: 1955).

13. Munford, *Virginia's Attitude toward Slavery and Secession,* 163, citing *William Lloyd Garrison by his children*, Vol. 1, 253-54.

14. "Inflation Calculator," accessed 2018. According to the Morgan-Friedman Inflation Calculator, $20 in 1833 was worth $515.29 in 2017 dollars.

15. Livingston, "Why the War Was Not about Slavery," 7–8.

16. Munford, *Virginia's Attitude toward Slavery and Secession,* 171.

17. Munford, *Virginia's Attitude toward Slavery and Secession,* 171-72, citing Williams, *History of the Negro Race in America*, Vol. II, 123, *Illinois Convention Journal*, 1862, 1098.

18. Munford, *Virginia's Attitude toward Slavery and Secession,* 171.

19. Kennedy and Kennedy, *The South Was Right!*, 55; Munford, *Virginia's Attitude toward Slavery and Secession,* 171.

20. Munford, *Virginia's Attitude toward Slavery and Secession,* 172.

21. Livingston, "Why the War Was Not about Slavery," 7, citing Eugene Berwanger, *The Frontier Against Slavery* (Urbana, Illinois: 1967).

22. Kennedy and Kennedy, *The South Was Right!*, 56; Mildred L. Rutherford, *Truths of History* (Athens, Georgia: 1907), 92. The Northwest of 1862 is today's Midwest.

23. Munford, *Virginia's Attitude toward Slavery and Secession,* 167, citing "General Sherman's Letters Home," *Scribner's Magazine* (April 1909), 400.

24. Livingston, "Why the War Was Not about Slavery," 16. Wade (1800–1878) served in the Senate from 1851 to 1869. He led the fight to impeach President Andrew Johnson in 1867-68. Wade was president pro tempore of the Senate at the time and would have become president if Johnson had been impeached, since there was no vice president (the law making the Speaker of the House next in

line was not enacted until 1947). The thought of Wade as president saved Johnson in part. So radical was the Republican Party at this time that several prominent Republican leaders urged then presidential candidate Ulysses S. Grant to pick Wade as his vice presidential candidate. Grant picked Schuyler Colfax instead. Wade was defeated for reelection in late 1868.

25. Dr. Richard Gatling was from North Carolina.
26. Wilson, "Those People, Part II," 58, 72.
27. Jennings C. Wise, *The Long Arm of Lee* (Lynchburg, Virginia: 1915; reprint ed., Harrisburg, Pennsylvania: 1995), 32–33.
28. Tom Paone, "Plans for the Little Known Confederate Helicopter." https:// airandspace.si.edu/stories/editorial/plans-little-known-confederate-helicopter. Mr. Paone was a museum specialist in the Aeronautics Department of the Air and Space Museum in 2013.
29. Kennedy, *Poverty*, 30, citing Frank L. Owsley, *Plain Folk of the Old South* (Baton Rouge: 1949), 86.
30. Hummel, *Emancipating Slaves, Enslaving Free Men*, 315.
31. William Cawthon, "Was the South Poor Before the War?" Abbeville Institute, May 26, 2017, Table II, 27. This essay was originally entitled "The Affluent Section: The South on the Eve of the War Between the States," and was written in 1982 under the direction of Emory Thomas at the University of Georgia. The figures are from the Census of 1860 and include slaves as potential wealthholders.
32. Dr. Charles Aiken, University of Tennessee, 1979 lecture.
33. Wilson, "Those People," 53.
34. James P. Reger, *Life in the South During the Civil War* (San Diego, California: 1997), 59.

Chapter VII: Agitation and Compromise

1. William Lloyd Garrison, "The Insurrection," *The Liberator*, September 3, 1831.
2. Arthur Tappen (1786-1865) was the brother of Ohio Senator Benjamin Tappen.
3. Hummel, *Emancipating Slaves, Enslaving Free Men*, 21.
4. Ibid., 25.
5. Ibid., 22-23.
6. Nehemiah Adams, *A South-side View of Slavery Or, Three Months at the South in 1854* (Bedford, Massachusetts: 1854), 108.
7. Ibid., 106-08.
8. Ibid., 108.
9. Wilson, "Those People," 52.
10. From the article "John Tyler, Son of Virginia," *Confederate Veteran Magazine*, Volume XXIV (1916), 4–5.
11. Hummel, *Emancipating Slaves, Enslaving Free Men*, 87. Wilmot did vote to annex Texas as a slave state because slavery was already established there.
12. Hummel, *Emancipating Slaves, Enslaving Free Men*, 88.
13. James G. Blaine, *Twenty Years of Congress: From Lincoln to Garfield* (Norwick, Connecticut: 1884), Volume I, 272.
14. Hummel, *Emancipating Slaves, Enslaving Free Men*, 55.

15. Ludwell H. Johnson, *North Against South* (New York: 1978; reprint ed., Columbia, S.C.: 1993), 23.
16. James K. Polk (1795–1849) was a much better president than he is commonly given credit for being. He promised when he was elected to serve only one term. He died, reportedly of cholera, three months after he left office.
17. Cass's running mate was Major General William O. Butler, who had been Taylor's second-in-command at the Battle of Buena Vista. He was a Congressman in 1848.
18. Hummel, *Emancipating Slaves, Enslaving Free Men*, 90.
19. Henry Clay was born in Hanover County, Virginia, on April 12, 1777, and died of tuberculosis on June 29, 1852. His will freed the slaves he owned at the time of his death. Despite all his activities, he found time to father 11 children. His second cousin, Cassius Marcellus Clay, was one of the leading abolitionists in Kentucky.
20. Johnson, *North Against South*, 17.
21. Webster died on October 24, 1852.
22. Hummel, *Emancipating Slaves, Enslaving Free Men*, 55.
23. Hummel, *Emancipating Slaves, Enslaving Free Men*, 95, citing Herbert Mitgang, ed., *Abraham Lincoln: A Press Portrait* (Chicago: 1971), 373.
24. Preston Brooks (1819–57) attended South Carolina College, but the college expelled him for threatening local police officers with firearms. He fought a duel with Louis T. Wigfall (future senator from Texas) in 1840. Shot in the hip, Brooks had to use a walking cane the rest of his life. He nevertheless fought in the Mexican War. He served in the South Carolina House of Representatives before election to Congress in 1852.

Chapter VIII: The Chasm Grows

1. Levi Woodbury (b. 1789) was the former governor and U.S. senator from New Hampshire. He had also served as secretary of the navy and secretary of the treasury under Jackson and Van Buren.
2. The Pierces had two other sons, both of whom died young.
3. Hummel, *Emancipating Slaves, Enslaving Free Men*, 105.
4. Allan Nevins, *Ordeal of the Union: A House Dividing* (New York: 1947), Vol. I, 111.
5. Hummel, *Emancipating Slaves, Enslaving Free Men*, 86.
6. Ibid., 110.
7. The Wyandotte Constitution is still the law of the land in Kansas, although it was amended many times.
8. Livingston, "Why the War Was Not about Slavery," 18.
9. Hummel, *Emancipating Slaves, Enslaving Free Men*, 112.
10. Edwin E. Sparks, ed., *The Lincoln-Douglas Debates* (Dansville, New York: 1918), 76–77; Harold Holzer, ed., *The Lincoln-Douglas Debates: The First Complete, Unexpurgated Text* (New York: 1993), 356–57.

Chapter IX: John Brown, Terrorist and Lightning Rod

1. George Edmonds (pseudonym for Mary Elizabeth Avery Meriwether), *Facts and Falsehoods Concerning the War on the South, 1861-1865* (Memphis: 1904), 180 (hereafter cited as "Edmonds").

2. Stuart named his second child Philip St. George Cooke after his father-in-law.

3. Burke Davis, *Jeb Stuart: The Last Cavalier* (New York: 1957; reprint ed., New York: 2000), 40-41.

4. Johnson, *North Against South*, 57.

5. James M. McPherson, *The Battle Cry of Freedom* (Oxford: 2003), 205.

6. Dowdey, *Lee*, 119.

7. Beckman owned five slaves until his death. His will freed them.

8. Turner (b. 1814) was a member of the class of 1831. Lee graduated in 1829. Turner was commissioned second lieutenant of artillery on graduation and served as an assistant professor of mathematics at West Point (1831–32). Posted to Charleston, South Carolina, during the Nullification Crisis, later, he did garrison duty in Connecticut and North Carolina, and saw action in Florida against the Seminoles. Turner resigned from the army in 1836. He was engaged in farming at the time of his death.

9. William Edward Burghardt Du Bois, *John Brown* (Philadelphia: 1909), 332.

10. Dowdey, *Lee*, 119.

11. Du Bois, *John Brown*, 333ff. 34. The exact details of the fight in the firehouse vary slightly.

12. Israel Greene (1824–1909) was born in Plattsburgh, New York but grew up in Wisconsin. His wife, however, was a Virginian. He joined the Marine Corps, trained in the artillery at West Point, and was named commander of the Marine Barracks in Washington, D.C., in April 1859. When the Civil War broke out, Greene was offered a lieutenant colonelcy in the Virginia infantry or a colonelcy in the Wisconsin militia. Instead, he joined the Confederate marines as a captain. Eventually promoted to major, he remained in Richmond throughout the war and was captured during the retreat to Appomattox. He moved to Mitchell, Dakota Territory, in 1873, where he was a farmer, civil engineer, and surveyor. He died at his farm near Mitchell.

13. This was Jeremiah G. Anderson, age twenty-six, who died of his wound.

14. Dowdey, *Lee*, 119.

15. John Taylor, "'What We Have To Expect': The Extradition Cases and Secession," in *To Live and Die in Dixie*, ed. Frank B. Powell, III (Columbia, Tennessee: 2014), 220, citing William W. Freehling, *The Road to Disunion: Secessionists Triumphant, 1854-1861* (New York: 2007), 220.

16. Du Bois, *John Brown*, 353.

17. Wilson, "Those People," 42.

18. Dowdey, *Lee*, 119.

19. Hummel, *Emancipating Slaves, Enslaving Free Men*, 121.

20. Huger William Johnstone, *Truth of the War Conspiracy of 1861* (Idylwild, Georgia: 1921), 20.

21. Stearns died in Florence, Italy, on May 10, 1860.

22. Higginson (1823–1911) was also active in the women's rights movement. He later commanded the 1st (U.S.) South Carolina Infantry, America's first African-American regiment. His book *Army Life in a Black Regiment* (1870) has been published online by Project Gutenberg (Gutenberg.org). He resigned his colonelcy due to wounds in October 1864.

23. Taylor, "'What We Have To Expect,'" 217.

24. Ibid.

Chapter X: The Election of 1860

1. Scruggs, "The Morrill Tariff," 139, citing Karl Marx and Friedrich Engels, *The Civil War in the United States* (reprint ed., New York: 1937), 58.

2. Today, federal elections are held in November, except for special elections, which can occur at any time.

3. Hummel, *Emancipating Slaves, Enslaving Free Men*, 118.

4. See Sara Agnes Rice Pryor, *Reminiscences of Peace and War* (New York: 1905). Mrs. Pryor was the wife of Congressman Roger A. Pryor, a Washington insider.

5. Cushing (1800–1879) was a former member of Congress, ambassador to China, brigadier general in the Mexican War, and US attorney general in the Pierce administration. Twice, he was the Democratic nominee for governor of Massachusetts but was unsuccessful both times in the general election.

6. Benjamin Fitzpatrick (1802–69) was the former governor of Alabama (1841–45) and U.S. senator (1848–49 and 1853–61). He did not hold higher office in the Confederacy, although he was president of the Alabama Constitutional Convention in 1865.

7. Herschel V. Johnson (1812–80) was later a Confederate senator (1863–65).

8. As a consolation prize of sorts, Lincoln appointed Bates U.S. attorney general.

9. John Bell (1796–1869) was a slave owner, but he opposed the expansion of slavery. He was a member of the Tennessee Senate (1817–21), the US House of Representatives (1827–41), and the U.S. Senate (1847–59). He briefly served as U.S. secretary of war in 1841. Bell voted against admitting Kansas to the Union under the Lecompton Constitution, prompting the Tennessee legislature to demand his resignation, but he refused to submit it and finished his second term. He met with Lincoln in March 1861. The president assured him that he would not use force vis-à-vis Fort Sumter. Bell felt deceived after the Union forces tried to reinforce the fort. He endorsed the Confederacy on April 23, 1861 and withdrew from politics.

10. Hummel, *Emancipating Slaves, Enslaving Free Men*, 131.

11. Livingston, "Why the War Was Not about Slavery," 19.

12. Albert Taylor Bledsoe, *Is Davis a Traitor or Was Secession a Constitutional Right?* (1866; reprint ed., Richmond: 1907).

Chapter XI: The Real Cause of the War

1. Paul Yarborough, *"Why Lee? Why Action?"* The Abbeville Blog, The Abbeville Institute, March 31, 2017.

2. Shelby Foote, Interview with Kevin Mieszala, September 2, 2001. Available on YouTube.

3. Kennedy and Kennedy, *The South Was Right!,* 48.

4. Raphael Semmes, *Memories of Service Afloat,* (Baltimore: 1869), 57–59.

5. Hummel, *Emancipating Slaves, Enslaving Free Men,* 39.

6. Lyon G. Tyler, *A Confederate Catechism* (Athens, Georgia: 1935), 6.

7. Rutherford, 12.

8. Scruggs, "The Morrill Tariff," 137.

9. Livingston, "Why the War Was Not about Slavery," 3.

10. Scruggs, "The Morrill Tariff," 137.

11. Ibid., 138.

12. Edmonds, *Facts and Falsehoods,* 58.

13. Donn Piatt, *Memories of the Men Who Saved the Union* (New York and Chicago: 1887), 30. Piatt (born 1819) was a lawyer, judge, diplomat, and author from Ohio. Piatt was a fervent abolitionist. His time as a Lincoln advisor was short. As temporary commander of Union forces in Maryland in 1861, Colonel Piatt ordered the recruiting of an African-American brigade. Only slaves could enlist. This led to a stormy scene in the White House, with Lincoln threatening him with a dishonorable discharge. Secretary of War Stanton intervened on his behalf, and he stayed in the army, though barred from further promotion until the end of the war, when he was brevetted brigadier general. He won election to the Ohio legislature as a Republican after the war. See Henry Howe, *Historical Collections of Ohio* (Norwalk, Ohio: 1888), Volume II, 113-15.

14. Scruggs, "The Morrill Tariff," 138.

15. Ibid., 158.

16. This point is arguable.

17. Spence, *The American Union,* 190.

18. R. W. Fogle and S. L. Engerman, *Time on the Cross* (Boston: 1974), 248-56.

19. Edmonds, *Facts and Falsehoods,* 170.

20. Ibid., 164.

21. Howard Cecil Perkins, ed., *Northern Editorials on Secession* (Gloucester, Massachusetts: 1964), Vol. I, 335.

22. Ibid., 331.

23. Ibid., 348.

24. Ibid., 355.

25. Ibid., 359.

26. Ibid., Vol. 2, 591–92.

27. Ibid., 598–99.

Chapter XII: Lincoln and His Agenda

1. Johnstone, *Truth of the War Conspiracy of 1861,* 32.

2. Thomas Landess, "The Dark Side of Abraham Lincoln," *The Abbeville Review,* December 10, 2015.

3. Clyde Wilson, "Those People," 41.

4. Walter D. Kennedy, *Rekilling Lincoln* (Gretna, Louisiana: 2015), 147.

5. See https://en.wikipedia.org/wiki/Religious_affiliations_of_Presidents_of_the_
    United_States. Ward Hill Lamon (1828-1893) was a lawyer, Lincoln's
    bodyguard, a US marshal, and a close friend of the president from their
    Springfield days. Lincoln sent him on a mission to Richmond, Virginia, in April
    1865, so he was not available to protect Lincoln the night John Wilkes Booth
    assassinated him. William Herndon (1818-1891) was Lincoln's law partner and
    early biographer. See William Henry Herndon and Jesse William Weik,
    Abraham Lincoln (Chicago: 1889 and 1896), three volumes, two of which have
    been reprinted online by Project Gutenberg. See http://www.gutenberg.org/
    ebooks/author/39490.

6. Ward H. Lamon, *Recollections of Abraham Lincoln, 1847–1865,* (Washington,
    D.C.: 1911), 335.

7. Matthew 12:25.

8. Brion McClanahan, "Washington vs. Lincoln," The Abbeville Blog, Abbeville
    Institute, February 22, 2017.

9. John W. Bell, *Memoirs of Governor William Smith of Virginia* (New York:
    1891), 402–03.

10. Munford, *Virginia's Attitude toward Slavery and Secession,* 168, citing
    Abraham Lincoln, Speeches, Letters and State Papers, N & H, Vol. I, 457–58.

11. Piatt, *Memories of the Men Who Saved the Union*31.

12. "Mystery Files: Abraham Lincoln," directed by Kent Haddock. Smithsonian
    Channel, 2015.

13. John M. Taylor, *Union at All Costs* (St. Petersburg, Florida: 2017), 31 (hereafter
    cited as "Taylor, *Union*"); David Herbert Donald, *Lincoln Reconsidered* (New
    York: 2001), 3.

14. Taylor, *Union,* 36; Charles L. C. Minor, *The Real Lincoln* (Richmond: 1901),
    36–37.

15. Ward H. Lamon, *Recollections of Abraham Lincoln, 1847–1865* (Washington,
    DC: 1911), 171.

16. Piatt, *Memories of the Men Who Saved the Union,* 30.

17. Edmonds, *Facts and Falsehoods,* 18–19.

18. Ibid., 13.

19. Walter Donald Kennedy, personal communication, 2019.

20. James McPherson, interviewed on Mystery Files: Abraham Lincoln, directed by
    Kent Haddock, Smithsonian Channel, 2015.

21. Seward, who was still in the Senate at that time, introduced the bill in the upper
    chamber.

22. Buchanan's signature was not necessary, but he signed it anyway, to lend it his
    support.

23. Spooner (1808–87), an entrepreneur and political philosopher, lived and died in
    Massachusetts. He ran a private mail delivery service in the 1840s, but the U.S.
    postmaster general used extralegal measures to drive him out of business. The
    government bombarded his company with harassing lawsuits until it could no
    longer afford to remain in operation. Having seen firsthand the power of an
    unbridled Federal government, Spooner became and remained a "small
    government" advocate for the rest of his life.

24. Spooner nevertheless recognized the South's right to secede.

25. Lysander Spooner, *No Treason: The Constitution of No Authority* (San Francisco: 1870), 1.

26. Ibid., 73.

27. Ibid., 79.

28. James Ronald Kennedy and Walter Donald Kennedy, *Was Jefferson Davis Right?* (Gretna, Louisiana: 1998), 291; James Ronald Kennedy, "Lincoln, Federal Supremacy, and the Death of States' Rights," in *To Live and Die in Dixie,* ed. Frank B. Powell, III (Columbia, Tennessee: 2014).

Chapter XIII: Over the Edge

1. E. B. Long, *The Civil War Day by Day* (New York: 1971), 3–4.

2. John Marquardt, "The Pickens Plot," The Abbeville Blog, The Abbeville Institute: April 23, 2018.

3. Lieutenant Commander Richard Rush and Robert H. Woods, *Official Records of the Union and Confederate Navies in the War of the Rebellion* (Washington, D.C.: 1880-1891), Series I, Volume 4, 90. Robert N. Scott, chief compiler, *The War of the Rebellion: A Complication of the Official Records of the Union and Confederate Armies* (Washington, DC: 1880–1891), Series I, Vol. I, 2. All *War of Rebellion* entries are Series I unless otherwise stated.

4. James G. Blaine, *Twenty Years of Congress: From Lincoln to Garfield,* (Norwick, Connecticut: 1884, 1886), Vol. I, 273.

5. Ibid., 273–74.

6. John B. Floyd (1806–63) was the former governor of Virginia (1848–1852). Later a Confederate general, he was forever tarnished by the debacle at Fort Donelson in February 1862.

7. Karen Stokes, "Fort Sumter and the Siege of Charleston," in *To Live and Die in Dixie,* ed. Frank B. Powell, III (Columbia, Tennessee: 2014), 164.

8. An eight-year congressman, Thompson was later a colonel in the Confederate Secret Service.

9. *The Constitution of the Confederate States of America* (Bedford, Massachusetts: n.d.), Article I, Section 7, Subsection 2.

10. Livingston, "Confederate Emancipation," 467.

11. Johnstone, *Truth of the War Conspiracy*, 16.

12. Wilson, "Those People II," 67.

13. Johnstone, *Truth of the War Conspiracy*, 11; Rush and Woods, *Official Records of the Union*, Vol. IV, 90; Scott, *The War of Rebellion*, Volume I, 352.

14. Henry Allen Adams (1800–1869) joined the navy as a midshipman at age thirteen and served in it for the next forty-eight years. He was a captain by 1855 and served as Admiral Perry's chief of staff when he opened Japan to the Western world. Later, he was part of the early naval blockade of Southern ports. Adams, promoted to commodore, retired in 1862.

15. Rush and Woods, *Official Records of the Union*, Vol. IV, 119.

16. Ibid., 110.

17. Johnstone, *Truth about the War Conspiracy*, 12. Johnstone (1844–1924) joined the army as a drummer boy in the 5th Georgia Infantry Regiment in 1861. He

later served in the 21st Georgia Cavalry Battalion and 7th Georgia Cavalry Regiment, fought throughout the war, and surrendered at Appomattox. "Introduction" by Charles Kelly Barrow, in the 2012 edition of Johnstone's book.

18. Rush and Woods, *Official Records of the Union*, Vol. IV, 110.
19. Stephen Mallory would be the Confederate secretary of the navy throughout the war.
20. William Henry Chase (1798–1870) was promoted to major general by the Florida Secession Convention and was commander of the "Army of Florida." A native of Massachusetts, his mother was the niece of John Hancock. He graduated from West Point in 1815 and remained in the army until 1856. By 1861, he was a major slaveholder and president of the Alabama and Florida Railroad Company. Ironically, Chase had designed and constructed Fort Pickens. Superseded by General Bragg as commander of the Southern forces at Pensacola on March 11, he took no further active part in the war. Bruce S. Allardice, *More Generals in Gray* (Baton Rouge: 1995), 56–57.
21. Rush and Woods, *Official Records of the Union*, Vol. IV, 110.
22. Johnstone, *Truth about the War Conspiracy*, 12. Israel Vogdes (1816–1889) was a West Point graduate (1837) and career army officer. Captured during the Battle of Santa Rosa Island (a Union victory) in 1862 and exchanged, later he was promoted to brigadier general, fighting in Florida, South Carolina, and Virginia. Ironically, H. W. Johnstone was one of the men who captured him at Santa Rosa by pulling him off a mule.
23. Gustavus V. Fox (1821–1883) was a U.S. naval officer during the Mexican War. Lincoln appointed him assistant secretary of the navy on August 1, 1861, a post he held until the end of the war.
24. Rush and Woods, *Official Records of the Union*, Vol. IV, 225.
25. Montgomery Blair (1813–1883) was a lawyer and part of an influential Missouri political family. He graduated from West Point in 1835, fought in the Seminole War in 1836, but then left the army and became a US district attorney and a judge. He moved to Maryland and set up a successful law practice in 1852. After the war, he fell out with the Radical Republicans and joined the Democrats. He ran for Congress in 1882 but was unsuccessful.
26. Rush and Woods, *Official Records of the Union*, Vol. IV, 223. Letter from Fox to General Scott.
27. Thomas Di Lorenzo, Interview on Confederate Broadcasting, aired April 18, 2018.
28. Perkins, ed., *Northern Editorials on Secession,* Vol. I, 361, citing editorial of March 11, 1861. The *True American* supported Douglas in the election of 1860.
29. Rush and Woods, *Official Records of the Union*, Vol. IV, 244–51.
30. Johnstone, *Truth about the War Conspiracy*, 16; Alexander H. Stephens, *A Constitutional View of the Late War Between the States* (Philadelphia: 1868), Vol. II, 354.
31. Johnstone, *Truth about the War Conspiracy*, 14; Stephens, Vol. II, 743–46.
32. Johnstone, *Truth about the War Conspiracy*, 16.
33. Ibid., 16.

34. Rush and Woods, *Official Records of the Union*, Vol. IV, 247.

35. Ibid., 227–28.

36. Johnstone, *Truth about the War Conspiracy*, 18-19.

37. Stephen C. Rowan (1808-1890) was born in Dublin, Ireland. He joined the U.S. Navy in 1826 and served until 1889, retiring as a vice admiral.

38. Rush and Woods, *Official Records of the Union*, Vol. IV, 107–08.

39. Ibid., 108.

40. Rev. R. L. Dabney, "Memoir of a Narrative Received of Colonel John B. Baldwin, of Staunton, Touching on the Origin of the War," *Southern Historical Society Papers*, Volume 1 (June 1876), 443 (hereafter cited as "Baldwin Interview").

41. Ibid., 445.

42. John Brown Baldwin (1820-1873) was born in Staunton and lived there his entire life. He attended the University of Virginia, became a lawyer, a militia officer, and was a state representative from 1848-1861. See Allardice, 50–51.

43. Dabney, "Memoir of a Narrative," 446.

44. Ibid., 447.

45. Ibid., 447.

46. Johnstone, *Truth about the War Conspiracy*, 22.

47. Dabney, "Memoir of a Narrative," 451.

48. Scruggs, "The Morrill Tariff," 144, citing Robert L. Dabney, "The True Purposes of the Civil War" and "Memoir of a Narrative Received of Colonel John Baldwin," Discussions Volume IV *Secular* (Mexico, 1897; reprint ed., Harrisonburg, Virginia: 1994).

49. Dabney, "Memoir of a Narrative," 451.

50. Baldwin related the story of his interview with Lincoln to Colonel Dabney in a Confederate earthwork in March 1865. Dabney double-checked the facts with Alexander H. H. Stuart, another pro-Union Virginian and Baldwin's law partner. Stuart confirmed that the story was as Baldwin related it to the Virginia peace delegation in April 1861. He independently confirmed other parts of the article.

51. Stokes, "Fort Sumter," 165-66. Also see John S. Tilley, *Lincoln Takes Command: How Lincoln Got the War He Wanted* (Chicago: 1941).

52. James H. Street, *The Civil War* (New York: 1953), 34 (hereafter cited as "Street").

53. Stephens, Volume II, 744.

54. Johnstone, *Truth*, 39.

55. Mary Chesnut, *Mary Chesnut's Civil War*, ed. C. Vann Woodward (New Haven, Connecticut and London: 1981), 48.

56. Ibid., 45.

57. O.R., Vol. I, 12.

58. Baldwin Interview, 452.

59. Hummel, 141.

60. Alexander Hugh Holmes Stuart (1807–1891) was a prominent lawyer and statesman. He had served in both houses of the Virginia legislature, in the U.S. Congress, and as secretary of the interior under Fillmore and Pierce. He refused

to hold any offices during the war, although he supported relief efforts for Confederate soldiers. He was a cousin of Confederate Generals Jeb Stuart and John B. Baldwin. He served in the Virginia General Assembly after Reconstruction.

61. Scott, *The War of the Rebellion,* Series 3, Vol. I, 76.
62. Scruggs, "The Morrill Tariff," 144. Colonel Baldwin became a staff officer of Virginia State Troops in April 1861, and commander of the 52nd Virginia Infantry Regiment in August 1861. He was a member of the Confederate Congress, 1862–65. He returned to the state legislature after the war and became speaker of the House. He died in 1873 at age fifty-three. His brother was Lieutenant Colonel Briscoe Baldwin, the chief ordnance officer of the Army of Northern Virginia.
63. E. B. Long, *The Civil War Day by Day,* (New York: 1971), 77.
64. Johnstone, *Truth about the War Conspiracy,* 32.
65. "Winston Churchill Quotes," Brainy Quotes, https://www.brainyquote.com/quotes/winston_churchill_380864.
66. Egon Richard Tausch, "The American Dream: North and South (and What Became of It)" in *To Live and Die in Dixie,* ed. Frank B. Powell, III (Columbia, Tennessee: 2014), 401. Samuel Wylie Crawford, *The Genesis of the Civil War: The Story of Sumter 1860–1861* (New York: 1887), 420.
67. Francis Key Howard, *Fourteen Months in the American Bastiles* (London: 1863), 9. Howard (1826–72) was also the grandson of Colonel John Eager Howard, Revolutionary War hero and commander of the 2nd Regiment of the Maryland Line, Continental Army. He later served as governor of Maryland and U.S. senator. Francis Howard was editor of the Daily Exchange, a Baltimore newspaper, and arrested at his home in the dead of night for criticizing Lincoln for suspending the writ of habeas corpus.

Chapter XIV: Tyranny and Emancipation

1. Clyde Wilson, *The Yankee Problem: An American Dilemma* (Columbia, South Carolina: 2016), 78.
2. Thomas DiLorenzo, *The Real Lincoln,* (New York: 2002), 252.
3. Rev. A. D. Betts, W. A. Betts, ed., *Experiences of a Confederate Chaplain, 1861–1864* (Greenville, S.C.: n.d), 6. (Online edition courtesy of the University of North Carolina, Chapel Hill). A. D. Betts, who was born in 1832 and died in 1918, was chaplain for the 30th North Carolina.
4. "Patrick Cleburne Quotes," AZ Quotes, www.azquotes.com/author/35953-Patrick_Cleburne. Cleburne rose to the rank of major general before being killed in action on November 30, 1864, in the Battle of Franklin, Tennessee.
5. Ibid.
6. Robert Stiles, *Four Years Under Marse Robert* (New York and Washington: 1910), 49–50.
7. Hunter McGuire and George L. Christian, *The Confederate Cause and Conduct in the War Between the States* (Richmond: 1907), 22.
8. See James M. McPherson, *For Cause and Comrades: Why Men Fought in the Civil War* (New York and Oxford: 1997), 13, 104–06.

9. Thomas H. Hicks (1798–1865) was elected governor in 1858 in an election noted for its corruption, open intimidation of voters, and violence. Hicks was a member of the Constitutional Union Party at the time. At other times, he was a Democrat, Whig, American (Know Nothing), and a Republican. He was later a U.S. senator (December 1862–1865).

10. Hummel, *Emancipating Slaves, Enslaving Free Men*, 142.

11. Thomas DiLorenzo, *Lincoln Unmasked* (New York: 2006; reprint ed., New York: 2006), 93, citing Frederick S. Calhoun, *The Lawmen: United States Marshals and Their Deputies, 1789–1989*.

12. Despite a lack of military training, John C. Breckinridge eventually became a pretty effective Confederate general.

13. Kennedy and Kennedy, *The South Was Right!*, 28.

14. Edgar Lee Masters, *Lincoln the Man* (1931; reprint ed., Columbia, South Carolina: 1997), 411.

15. Edmonds, *Facts and Falsehoods*, 213.

16. Wilson, "Those People II," 70.

17. Livingston, "Why the War Was Not about Slavery," 8.

18. Wilson, "Those People II," 64, citing Douglass, "Oration in Memory of Abraham Lincoln," Washington, D.C., April 14, 1876.

19. Sam Watkins, *Co Aytch* (reprint ed., New York: 1970), 244.

20. David H. Donald, Jean Harvey Baker, and Michael F. Holt, *Civil War and Reconstruction* (New York: 2001), 315.

21. Kennedy and Kennedy, *The South Was Right!*, 26.

22. Sherman held slaves when he lived in Louisiana in 1860. It is unclear if he carried them north when the war began. It is certain, however, that he had no problem with slavery.

23. Piatt, *Memories of the Men*, 150.

24. Spooner, *No Treason*, 73.

25. Kennedy, "Federal Supremacy," 197.

26. The Emancipation Proclamation was issued on September 22, 1862 but was to take effect on January 1, 1863.

27. Morgan Friedman Inflation Calculator.

28. James Howell Street, *The Civil War* (New York, 1953), 90.

29. Herbert Asbury, *The Gangs of New York* (New York: 1928), 169.

30. E. B. Long, 384.

31. Norman Black, "A Return to Barbarism," The Abbeville Blog, Abbeville Institute, November 12, 2018; Ezra J. Warner, *Generals in Blue* (Baton Rouge: 1864), 511–12. Turchin, who was born in 1822, died in an insane asylum in Illinois in 1901.

32. General McPherson was the commander of the XVII Corps in Grant's army at the time. He was commander of the Army of the Tennessee on July 22, 1864, when he was shot down and killed while trying to escape Confederate forces.

33. Elizabeth Meade Ingraham, "Diary." On file at the McCandle Library, Old City Courthouse Museum, Vicksburg, Mississippi.

34. Ibid.

35. Her husband, Colonel Jacob Thompson (1810–1885), was off fighting the Yankees. A former congressman and secretary of the interior, he directed the Canadian branch of the Confederate Secret Service and may have headed the entire organization. Prior to that, he served on the Western Front.
36. Samuel W. Mitcham, Jr., *Bust Hell Wide Open: The Life of Nathan Bedford Forrest* (Washington, D.C.: 2016), 232.
37. Ulysses Robert Brooks, *Butler and his Cavalry in the War of Secession, 1861–1865* (Columbia, South Carolina: 1909), 453–54.

Chapter XV: The Costs and Results of the War

1. Douglas Southall Freeman, *R. E. Lee*, Vol. IV (New York: 1935), 304. Lee wrote this to John E. E. Dalberg-Acton, Member of Parliament (later Lord Acton) of the United Kingdom, shortly after the war
2. Livingston, "Confederate Emancipation," 462.
3. Jim Downs, *Sick From Freedom: African-American Illness and Suffering During the Civil War and Reconstruction* (Oxford: 2012), 4–7.
4. Johnson, *North Against South,* 190.
5. Ibid., 189.
6. Livingston, "Confederate Emancipation," 459.
7. Ibid.
8. There were 225,961 free black people in the North in 1860, as opposed to 250,787 in the South. Southern Historical Society post 2017, citing the University of Virginia Library Geostat Historical Census Browser, http://fisher.lib.virginia.edu/collections/stats/histcensus.
9. Barnickel, *Milliken's Bend,* 54, citing *Freedom: A Documentary History of Emancipation, 1861–1867,* ed. Ira Berlin, Joseph P. Reidy, and Leslie S. Rowland, Series 2, *The Black Military Experiece* (Cambridge: 1982), 734–35.
10. Barnickel, *Milliken's Bend,* 119.
11. Scott, *The War of the Rebellion*, Series 2, Volume 6, 735.
12. One of these speculators was Lewis Dent, a brother-in-law of General Grant. The Rebels captured him but treated him well. When Confederate Brigadier General Paul O. Hebert, the commander of the Subdistrict of Northeast Louisiana, discovered who he was, he released him. He also sent a note to Grant, asking for the release of Major Semmes in exchange for Dent, a Confederate staff officer, who had been captured near Natchez. Grant promptly wrote to Washington, asking that Semmes be freed. Barnickel, *Milliken's Bend,* 119; Scott, *The War of the Rebellion*, Series 2, Volume VI, 194, letter from U.S Grant to Colonel William Hoffman, Commissary-General of Prisoners, Washington, D.C., August 11, 1863.
13. Jim Downs, *Sick from Freedom: African-American Death and Suffering during the Civil War and Reconstruction,* (Oxford: 2012), 8.
14. Livingston, "Confederate Emancipation," 462.
15. Hummel, *Emancipating Slaves, Enslaving Free Men,* 316; J. Mills Thornton, III, "Fiscal Policy and the Failure of Radical Reconstruction in the Lower South," in *Region, Race, and Reconstruction: Essays in Honor of C. Vann*

Woodward, ed. J. Morgan Kousser and James M. McPherson, (New York: 1982), 371.

16. See Philip Leigh, *U. S. Grant's Failed Presidency* (Columbia, South Carolina: 2019).

17. Hummel, *Emancipating Slaves, Enslaving Free Men*, 314.

18. See Kennedy and Kennedy, *Punished with Poverty*, 155-60.

19. For an excellent account of the Reconstruction era in the South, see Philip Leigh, *Southern Reconstruction* (Chicago: 2017).

BIBLIOGRAPHY

Abbeville Institute, abbevilleinstitute.org. Includes *The Abbeville Review* and *The Abbeville Blog*. Various issues.

Adams, Charles Francis. *When in the Course of Human Events: Arguing the Case for Southern Secession*. Boulder, Colorado, and London: 2000.

———. *Lee at Appomattox: And Other Papers*. Boston and New York: 2nd Edition (enlarged), 1902.

Adams, Nehemiah. *South-Side View of Slavery; or Three Months at the South, in 1854*. Bedford, Massachusetts: 1854.

Aiken, Charles. Lectures, University of Tennessee: 1979-1981.

Allardice, Bruce S. *Confederate Colonels*. Columbia, Missouri: 2008.

———. *More Generals in Gray*. Baton Rouge: 1995.

Allen, James S. *Reconstruction: The Battle for Democracy, 1865–1876*. New York: 1937.

Asbury, Herbert. *The Gangs of New York*. New York: 1928.

A-Z Quotes. www.azquotes.com.

Bailey, Thomas A., and David M. Kennedy. *The American Pageant*. 7th ed. 2 vols. Lexington, Massachusetts, and Toronto, Canada: 1983.

Barnickel, Linda. *Milliken's Bend*. Baton Rouge: 2013.

Beard, Charles A., and Mary R. Beard. *The Rise of American Civilization*. 2 vols. New York: 1927.

Bell, John W. *Memoirs of Governor William Smith of Virginia*. New York: 1891.

Berlin, Ira, Joseph P. Reidy, and Leslie S. Rowland, eds. *Freedom: A Documentary History of Emancipation, 1861–1867*. Series 2, *The Black Experience*. Cambridge: 1982.

Berwanger, Eugene. *The Frontier Against Slavery*. Urbana, Illinois: 1967.

Betts, A. D. [Alexander D.]. *Experiences of a Confederate Chaplain, 1861-1864*. Greenville, South Carolina: n.d. Online version courtesy University of North Carolina Chapel Hill. docsouth.unc.edu/fpn/betts/betts.html.

Black, Norman. "A Return of Barbarism," *The Abbeville Blog*, Abbeville Institute. November 12, 2018.

Blaine, James G. *Twenty Years of Congress: From Lincoln to Garfield*. 2 vols.Norwick, Connecticut: 1884 and 1886.

Bledsoe, Albert Taylor. *Is Davis a Traitor or Was Secession a Constitutional Right?* 1866. Reprint ed. Richmond: 1907.

Brooks, Ulysses Robert. *Butler and his Cavalry in the War of Secession, 1861-1865*. Columbia, South Carolina: 1909.

Burton, Sir Richard Francis. *A Mission to Gelele, King of Dahome*. London: 1864.

Canot, Theodore. *Captain Canot or Twenty Years of an African Slaver*. New York: 1854.

Cawthon, William. "Was the South Poor before the War?" Abbeville Institute, May 26, 2017.

Chesnut, Mary. *Mary Chesnut's Civil War*. Edited by C. Vann Woodward. New Haven, Connecticut, and London: 1981.

Cisco, Walter B. *War Crimes Against Southern Civilians*. Gretna, Louisiana: 2007.

Confederate Veteran Magazine. Various issues.

Constitution of the Confederate States of America. Bedford, Massachusetts: n.d.

Crawford, Samuel W. *The Genesis of the Civil War: The Story of Sumter, 1860–1861*. New York: 1887.

Crocker, H. W., III. *The Politically Incorrect Guide to the Civil War*. Washington, D.C.: 2008.

Dabney, Robert Lewis. "Baldwin's Interview with Lincoln—A Memoir." *Southern Historical Society Papers*, Vol. I (June 1876).

Dabney, Robert Lewis. *A Defense of Virginia: And Through Her, of the South*. New York: 1867.

Davis, Burke. *Jeb Stuart: The Last Cavalier*. New York: 1957. Reprint ed. New York: 2000.

DiLorenzo, Thomas. Interview on Confederate Broadcasting. Aired April 18, 2018, and periodically before and since.

———. *Lincoln Unmasked*. New York: 2006. Reprint ed. New York: 2006.

———. *The Real Lincoln*. New York: 2002. Reprint ed. New York: 2003.

Donald, David H. *Lincoln Reconsidered*. New York: 2001.

Donald, David H., Jean Harvey Baker, and Michael F. Holt. *Civil War and Reconstruction*. New York: 2001.

Dow, George Francis. *Slave Ships and Slaving*. Cambridge, Maryland: 1968.

Dowdey, Clifford. *Lee*. New York: 1965.

Downs, Jim. *Sick From Freedom: African-American Death and Suffering During the Civil War and Reconstruction*. Oxford: 2012.

Drake, Richard. *Revelations of a Slave Smuggler*. New York: 1860.

Du Bois, W. E. B. *John Brown*. Philadelphia: 1909.

———. *The Suppression of the African Slave-Trade to the United States of America, 1638-1870*. 1896. Reprint ed. New York: 1904.

Edmonds, George [pseudonym for Mary Elizabeth Avery Meriwether]. *Facts and Falsehoods Concerning the War on the South, 1861–1865*. Memphis: 1904.

Eicher, David J. *The Longest Night: A Military History of the Civil War*. New York: 2002.

Ellis, Edward S. *The Youth's History of the United States*. 2 vols. London: 1887.

Emison, John. "The Constitutionality of Secession." *To Live and Die in Dixie*. Edited by Frank B. Powell, III. Columbia, Tennessee: 2004.

Ewing, E. W. R. *Northern Rebellion and Southern Secession*. Richmond, Virginia: 1904.

Farrow, Anne, Joel Lang, and Jennifer Frank. *How the North Promoted, Prolonged and Profited from Slavery*. New York: 2005.

Fehrenbacher, Don E., ed. *Lincoln: Speeches and Writings*. New York: 1989.

Fischer, David H. *Albion's Seed*. Oxford: 1989.

Fogel, R. W., and S. L. Engerman. *Time on the Cross*. Boston: Little, Brown and Company, 1974.

Foote, Shelby. *The Civil War: A Narrative* Volume 3, *Red River to Appomattox*. New York: 1986.

———. "Interview." Posted on YouTube: 2016.

———. Interview with Kevin Mieszala, September 2, 2001. Available on YouTube.

Freehling, William W. *The Road to Disunion: Secessionists Triumphant, 1854–1861.* New York: 2007.

Freeman, Douglas Southall. *R. E. Lee.* 4 vols. New York: 1933, 1935.

Garrison, William Lloyd. "The Insurrection." *The Liberator,* September 3, 1831.

Gatell, Frank O., ed. *Essays on Jacksonian America.* New York: 1970.

Gates, Henry Lewis, Jr. "Ending the Slavery Blame-Game." *New York Times,* April 23, 2010. Also see https://www.nytimes.com/2010/04/23/opinion/23/gates.html.

Givens, R. Michael. "Introduction." *To Live and Die in Dixie.* Edited by Frank B. Powell, III. Columbia, Tennessee: 2004.

Green, Lorenzo Johnston. *The Negro in Colonial New England, 1620-1776.* Port Washington, New York: 1966.

Hedley, Joel Tyler. *The Great Riots of New York City.* New York: 1873.

Holzer, Harold, ed. *The Lincoln-Douglas Debates: The First Complete, Unexpurgated Text.* New York: 1993.

Horsmanden, Daniel. "The NY Conspiracy of 1741." The Gilder Institute of American History. https://gilderlehrman.org/content/new-york-conspiracy-1741.

Howard, Francis Key. *Fourteen Months in the American Bastiles.* London: 1863.

Howe, Henry. *Historical Collections of Ohio.* 2 vols. Norwalk, Ohio: 1888.

Hummel, Jeffrey R. *Emancipating Slaves, Enslaving Free Men.* Chicago: 1996.

Ingraham, Elizabeth Meade. "Diary." On file at the McCandles Library, Old City Courthouse, Vicksburg, Mississippi.

Jefferson, Thomas, letter to Abigail Adams, September 11, 1804. *www.robgagnon.net JeffersonOnJudicalTyranny.htm.*

"John Tyler, Son of Virginia." *Confederate Veterans Magazine,* XXIV (1916).

Johnson, Ludwell H. *North Against South.* New York: 1978. Reprint ed. Columbia, South Carolina: 1993.

Johnstone, Huger William. *Truth of the War Conspiracy of 1861.* Idylwild, Georgia: 1921.

Kennedy, James Ronald, and Walter Donald Kennedy. *Was Jefferson Davis Right?* Gretna, Louisiana: 1998.

———. *Punished with Poverty.* Columbia, South Carolina: 2016.

———. *The South Was Right!* 2nd ed. Gretna, Louisiana, 2004.

Kennedy, Walter Donald. *Rekilling Lincoln.* Gretna, Louisiana: 2015.

Kizer, Gene, Jr. *Slavery Was Not the Cause of the War Between the States.* Charleston, S.C.: 2014.

Kousser, Morgan and James M. McPherson, eds. *Region, Race, and Reconstruction: Essays in Honor of C. Vann Woodward.* New York: 1982.

Lamon, Ward H. *Recollections of Abraham Lincoln, 1847-1865.* Washington, DC: 1911.

Landess, Thomas. "The Dark Side of Abraham Lincoln." *The Abbeville Review.* December 10, 2015.

Leigh, Philip. *U. S. Grant's Failed Presidency.* Columbia, South Carolina: 2019.

———. *Southern Reconstruction.* Yardley, Pennsylvania: Westholme Publishing, 2017.

Lincoln, Abraham. "First Inaugural Address." March 4, 1861. Special Session, United States Senate, Executive Document No. 1. avalon.law.yale/edu/nineteenth century/lincoln1.asp. Yale Law School, Lillian Goldman Law Library, The Avalon Project.

Livingston, Donald W. "Confederate Emancipation Without War." *To Live and Die in Dixie.* Edited by Frank B. Powell, III. Columbia, Tennessee: 2004.

———. "Why the War Was Not About Slavery." *To Live and Die in Dixie.* Edited by Frank B. Powell, III. Columbia, Tennessee: 2004.

Long, E. B. *The Civil War Day by Day.* New York: 1971.

Mannix, Daniel P. *Black Cargoes.* New York: 1962.

Marquardt, John. "The Pickens Plot." *The Abbeville Blog*, The Abbeville Institute. April 23, 2018.

Marshall-Cornwall, James. *Grant as a Military Commander.* New York: 1970.

Marx, Karl and Friedrich Engels. *The Civil War in America.* Reprint ed. New York: 1937.

Masters, Edgar Lee. *Lincoln the Man.* 1931. Reprint ed. Columbia, South Carolina: 1997.

McClanahan, Biron. "Washington vs. Lincoln." *The Abbeville Blog.* Abbeville Institute: February 22, 2017.

McGuire, Hunter Holmes and George Llewellyn Christian. *Confederate Cause and Conduct in the War Between the States.* Richmond, Virginia: 1907.

McManus, Edgar J. *Black Bondage in the North.* Syracuse, New York: 1973.

———. *A History of Negro Slavery in New York.* Syracuse, New York: 2001.

McPherson, James M. *The Battle Cry of Freedom.* Oxford: 2003.

———. *For Cause and Comrades: Why Men Fought in the Civil War.* New York and Oxford: 1997.

———. *Ordeal by Fire: The Civil War and Reconstruction.* New York and Oxford: 1997.

———. Comments made on the television program *Mystery Files: Abraham Lincoln.* Directed by Kent Haddock. Smithsonian Channel.

McWhiney, Grady. "Jefferson Davis, the Unforgiven." *Journal of Mississippi History* XLII (May 1980).

Melish, Joanne Pope. *Disowning Slaver, Gradual Emancipation and Race in New England, 1780–1860.* Ithaca, New York: 1998.

Minor, Charles L. C. *The Real Lincoln.* Richmond: 1901.

Mitcham, Samuel W., Jr. *Bust Hell Wide Open: The Life of Nathan Bedford Forrest.* Washington, DC: 2016.

———. *Vicksburg.* Washington, DC: 2018.

Mitgang, Herbert, ed. *Abraham Lincoln: A Press Portrait.* Chicago: 1971.

Moore, George Henry. *Notes on the History of Slavery in Massachusetts.* New York: 1866. https://babel.hathitrust.org/cgi/pt?id=nyp.33433082 125349;view=1up;seq=8.

Morgan-Friedman Inflation Calculator. https://westegg.com/inflation/. Accessed 2018.

Morison, Samuel Eliot. *The Oxford History of the American People.* 3 vols. New York: 1972.

Munford, Beverly B. *Virginia's Attitude Toward Slavery and Secession.* 2nd School Edition. Richmond, Virginia: 1914.

Napolitano, Andrew P. *The Constitution in Exile.* Nashville, Tennessee: 2006.

Nevin, John. *John C. Calhoun and the Price of Union.* Baton Rouge, Louisiana: 1988.

Nevins, Allan. *Ordeal of the Union: A House Dividing.* New York: 1947.

Northup, Solomon, Sue Eakin, and Joseph Logsdon, eds. *Twelve Years a Slave.* Buffalo, New York and Cincinnati, Ohio: 1853. Reprint ed. Baton Rouge, Louisiana: 1975.

Oltman, Adele. "The Hidden History of Slavery in New York." *The Nation,* November 7, 2005.

Owsley, Frank L. *Plain Folk in the Old South.* Baton Rouge, Louisiana: 1949.

Paone, Tom. "Plans for the Little Known Confederate Helicopter." Posted January 23, 2013. https://airandspace.si.edu/stories/editorial/plans-little-known-confederate-helicopter

Perkins, Howard C., ed. *Northern Editorials on Secession.* 2 vols. Gloucester, Mass: 1964.

Piatt, Donn. *Memories of the Men Who Saved the Union.* New York and Chicago: 1887.

Pollard, Edward A. *The Lost Cause: A New Southern History of the War of the Confederates.* New York: 1867.

Powell, Frank B., III, ed. *To Live and Die in Dixie.* Columbia, Tennessee: 2004.

Powell, Jim. *The Greatest Emancipation: How the West Abolished Slavery.* New York: 2008.

Pryor, Sara Agnes Rice. *Reminiscences of Peace and War.* New York: 1905.

Preyer, Norris W. "Southern Support of the Tariff of 1816: A Reappraisal." *Journal of Southern History* XXV (August 1959).

Reger, James P. *Life in the South During the Civil War.* San Diego, California: 1997.

Rush, Richard and Robert H. Woods. *Official Records of the Union and Confederate Navies in the War of the Rebellion.* Washington, DC: 1894–1899.

Rutherford, Mildred L. *Truths of History.* Athens, Georgia: 1907.

Roesch, James Rutledge. *From Founding Fathers to Fire-Eaters: The Constitutional Doctrine of States' Rights in the Old South.* Columbia, South Carolina: 2018.

Schuckers, J. W. *The Life and Public Service of Salmon Portland Chase.* New York: 1874.

Scott, Robert N., chief comp. *The War of the Rebellion: A Complication of the Official Records of the Union and Confederate Armies.* Series 1. 128 vols. Washington, DC: 1880–1901.

———. *The War of the Rebellion: Complication of the Official Records of the Union and Confederate Armies.* Series 2. 5 vols. Washington, D.C.: 1880–1901.

Scott, Robert N., chief compiler. *The War of the Rebellion: Complication of the Official Records of the Union and Confederate Armies.* Series 3. 5 vols. Washington, D.C.: 1880–1901.

Scruggs, Leonard M. "The Morrill Tariff: Northern Provocation to Southern Secession." *To Live and Die in Dixie.* Edited by Frank B. Powell, III. Columbia, Tennessee: 2004.

Semmes, Raphael. *Memories of Service Afloat*. Baltimore: 1869.

Southern Historical Society Papers. Various Issues.

Sparks, Edwin E., ed. *The Lincoln-Douglas Debates*. Dansville, New York: 1918.

Spence, James. *The American Union*. 3rd ed. London: 1862.

Spooner, Lysander. *No Treason: The Constitution of No Authority*. 1870. Reprint ed. Free Patriot Press: n.d.

"Statistics on Slavery." faculty.weber.edu/kmackay/statistics_on_slavery.htm.

Stephens, Alexander H. *A Constitutional View of the Late War Between the States*. 2 vols. Philadelphia: 1868.

Street, James Howell. *The Civil War*. New York: 1953.

Stiles, Robert. *Four Years Under Marse Robert*. New York and Washington: 1910.

Stoddard, William O. *Volcano Under the City*. New York: 1887.

Stokes, Karen. "Fort Sumter and the Siege of Charleston." *To Live and Die in Dixie*. Edited by Frank B. Powell, III. Columbia, Tennessee: 2004.

Street, James H. *The Civil War*. New York: 1953.

Tausch, Egon Richard. "The American Dream: North and South (And What Became of It) ." *To Live and Die in Dixie*. Edited by Frank B. Powell, III. Columbia, Tennessee: 2004.

Taussig, Frank William. *History of the Present Tariff, 1860–1885*. New York and London: 1885.

The Tariff History of the United States. New York: 1888.

Taylor, John. "What We Have to Expect: The Extradition Cases and Secession." *To Live and Die in Dixie*. Edited by Frank B. Powell, III. Columbia, Tennessee: 2004.

Taylor, John M. *Union at All Costs*. St. Petersburg, Florida: 2017.

Thornton, J. Mills, III. "Fiscal Policy and the Failure of Radical Reconstruction in the Lower South." *Region, Race, and Reconstruction: Essays in Honor of C. Vann Woodward*. Edited by Morgan Kousser and James M. McPherson. New York: 1982.

Tilley, John S. *Lincoln Takes Command: How Lincoln Got the War He Wanted*. Chicago: 1941.

Tocqueville, Alexis de. *Democracy in America*. Editec by J. P. Manger. 1835. Reprint ed. New York: 1969.

Trask, H. A. Scott. "Who Won the Webster-Hayne Debate of 1830?" *The Abbeville Review*, Abbeville Institute, August 30, 2016.

Traywick, H. V., Jr. "Unlearning 'Fake History.'" *The Abbeville Blog.* The Abbeville Institute. April 25, 2018.

Tyler, Lyon G. *A Confederate Catechism.* Athens, Georgia: 1935.

United States Historical Tariff Collections. http://en.wikipedia.org/wiki/Tariffs_in_United_States_history.

Warner, Ezra J. *Generals in Blue.* Baton Rouge: 1964.

Watkins, Sam. *Co Aytch.* Reprint ed. New York: 1970.

Wilson, Clyde. *The Essential Calhoun: Selections from Writings, Speeches and Letters.* New Brunswich and London: 1992.

———. "'Those People'—Part I." *To Live and Die in Dixie.* Edited by Frank B. Powell, III. Columbia, Tennessee: 2004.

———. "'Those People'—Part II." *To Live and Die in Dixie.* Edited by Frank B. Powell, III. Columbia, Tennessee: 2004.

———. *The Yankee Problem: An American Dilemma.* Columbia, South Carolina: 2016.

Wilson, Dean. North Carolina State University lecture, 1973.

Wise, Jennings C. *The Long Arm of Lee.* 2 vols. Lynchburg, Virginia: 1915. Reprint ed. Harrisburg, Pennsylvania: 1995.

"Witchhunt in New York: The 1741 Rebellion." https://pbs.org/wgbh/aia/part1/1p256.html.

Woodward, C. Vann. *The Strange Career of Jim Crow.* New York: 1955.

Yarbrough, Paul. "Why Lee? Why Action?" *The Abbeville Blog.* Abbeville Institute: March 31, 2017.

INDEX